D0869175

SAVING MY FAMILY

Spiritual Warfare within My Home

Steve Koski

WESTBOW°
PRESS
A DIVISION OF THOMAS NELSON
& ZONDERVAN

Scripture taken from the New King James Version. Copyright 1979, 1980, 1982 by Thomas Nelson, inc. Used by permission. All rights reserved.

WestBow Press books may be ordered through booksellers or by contacting:

WestBow Press
A Division of Thomas Nelson & Zondervan
1663 Liberty Drive
Bloomington, IN 47403
www.westbowpress.com
1 (866) 928-1240

ISBN: 978-1-4908-4236-3 (sc)
ISBN: 978-1-4908-4237-0 (hc)
ISBN: 978-1-4908-4259-2 (e)

Printed in the United States of America.

Library of Congress Control Number: 2014911324

WestBow Press rev. date: 6/27/2014

To my loving family, Sharmalie, Danielle, and Aaron, and most importantly to all of our brothers and sisters saved by the blood of Christ and those yet to come.

Contents

Acknowledgments

New King James Version of the Holy Bible
Covenant Presbyterian Church in Woodbridge, VA
Knox and Bev Swayze, copastors (www.covenantpresbyterianchurch.us)
Minister Darrell and Cynthia Bailey
The blessed women who helped review content, Donna Motley and
   Jenn Sandoval
Alistair Begg from Truth for Life (truthforlife.org)
Billy Graham from Hour of Decision (billygraham.org)
Dennis Rainey and Bob Lepine from Family Life Today (familylife.com)
Dr. Charles Stanley from In Touch Ministries (intouch.org)
Dr. David Jeremiah from Turning Point (DavidJerimah.org)
Jack Graham from Power Point (jackgraham.org)
Jim Daily from Focus on the Family (focusonthefamily.com)
John MacArthur from Grace to You (gracechurch.org)
Joseph Prince from Joseph Prince Ministries (josephprince.org)
Michael Youssef from Leading the Way (leadingtheway.org)
R. C. Sproul from Renewing Your Mind (Ligonier.org)
Radio station WAVA 105.1 for Christian talk radio (wava.com)
Ravi Zacharias from Let My People Think (rzim.org)
Dr. Tony Evans from The Urban Alternative (tonyevens.org)

Preface

My family and I welcome all to share our journey to the Lord. Maybe your current situation has you looking for answers that might be found in our testing from the Lord, or maybe just need an encouraging word, which reminds you He *is* listening to your prayers, I'd like to pray that you find both in the pages of our book. I can guarantee that He is listening for your prayers, maybe thinking that you're not getting the answers you need or that your prayers are so improperly worded that He really doesn't understand what you want. Be assured that as the Bible states our Lord Jesus sits at the right hand of Father God, interceding on our behalf. He receives that mangled prayer that you send to Him and molds it into the perfect prayer and then presents it to the Father for an answer.

In our story—and indeed it was our trial—I had to gain knowledge of what exactly is the armor of God and how to apply it to my life and my family's situation. I would like to think that we are a practical example of putting on and wearing the entire armor of God. There are many experiences in our story that some may find hard to believe or even understand. I can comprehend this, but what I would like everyone to know right from the start is that all that is written and told by me in our book is true and happened as written.

I'd like to say at this point I have a real passion for the Lord. Sometimes it comes out with a warrior attitude in my writings and in speech because in our story that's how I had to react to _it_ (a demon), and that's who I became. This book was written after all of these events transpired. Really I believe and admire the true warriors, those who can pray for hours on end to the Lord, the so-called prayer warriors. I keep the Lord on my mind much more now than I did when our story began. He was pushing me to a point where I could be used to glorify Him and His work through our story. I hope and pray that I do Him this honor. Many of us wonder why we were created, why we are here, and what we are supposed to accomplish in life. I recently heard Dr. Tony Evans's sermon where he explained this quite well. In a nutshell he said that if your purpose furthers the Lord's kingdom or His name, then you're on the correct path to finding the calling, which you are supposed to accomplish. Wow, sound words of wisdom there. Maybe that means that this book is my life's calling. This is the reason I was put into this world, namely to tell our story so that someone else may benefit from our trials.

Also I have no formal religious education. I'm certainly not a scholar. In fact, I hope I spelled scholar right. I am just a student of the Bible like most. I will refer to myself as the pastor to my family in our story. I am referring to my biblical responsibilities to be the teacher to my family.

It is my sincere prayer that our book causes many to search out the true teachers of the Word of God. I have listed our favorites in the front of the book, those whom I believe teach the Word correctly. We hope to become a reason that brings new believers, or those who have strayed away, to Him through those teachers and resources listed. There are four of us in our family. I have asked each to write an addition to our story from their points of view in the hope that some who read this may find comments or ideas to help them solve some issue they are dealing with and discover the courage to continue to fight the evil that has invaded your home or family member. You must find the Word in the Bible that gathers strength in Him and call on all of heaven through Christ to fight your battle so that our heavenly Father releases His angels to answer your prayers. This can happen. Have faith, *strong* faith that our Lord Jesus is a man of His word, is able to do all, and does walk with you … *always*.

Yours in Christ,
Steve

CHAPTER 1

My Family

I wonder if the best place to start is at the end. Today through faith by the grace of God my immediate family—wife, son, and daughter—and I are saved by our Lord Jesus Christ. Our walk to Him was not short and certainly not easy. We have experienced blessings and trials that tested our very being and sanity, both from the Lord by visions and visitations as well as evil through demonic experiences, many of which I will relate to the reader in this book. The Bible states, "For we do not wrestle against flesh and blood, but against principalities, against powers, against the rulers of darkness of this age, against spiritual hosts of wickedness in heavenly places" (Ephesians 6:12).

It is this one verse that sets up our entire story. It states the challenge my family was about to face; however, it also is the very footing I needed to keep me based in the Word of the Bible and remember who the Enemy truly was in our struggle and who was really in control of everything. How do you know when you receive these visits from either good or evil? When truly experiencing spiritual events for the first time, it's so far out of the normal that you will understand what John said during his explanation of his revelation, "Immediately I was in the spirit." To those readers who have not yet come to call Jesus your Lord and Savior, John is one of the apostles of Jesus, and this passage refers to John being taken to heaven in spirit and shown what is to come in the end of the age, the end of the world as we know it today. Revelation is the last book of the Bible explaining what will be our future here on earth. I was also shown visions in this manner.

My name is Steve, husband of Sharmalie, my lovely wife, and father to Danielle, our firstborn, and Aaron, our son. We called them honorable number-one daughter and honorable number-one son, which worked out great because there was no sibling rivalry there! I was born and raised in Pittsburgh as the son of two of the greatest parents anyone could ask for. My father worked for a shipping company, packing boxes mostly, and my mother worked as a crossing guard for the kids during school transit hours. Being born and raised in the same home for all of my early life really gave me a sense of security. Actually my dad served in the US Air Force during the Korean War, and when he returned, he built the house that we lived in. During my early years we attended a Catholic church, but here's where that part of my life and my parents' lives really slipped. My dad and I would go every Sunday morning to pick up his mom, my grandmother, Bubby as we called her, and go to church in Braddock. Bubby would go downstairs during service and sit near the front to soak up as much as she could. Dad, my cousin Dave Terk (who was like a brother to me), and I would go to the balcony, where the organist played. Dave and I were both only children. We grew up very close and are even closer today through the bond of our Lord and our earthly family. I always tell everybody that I'm an only child because my parents reached perfection on the first try. Why try again? Dave and I would mostly screw around, and I could never tell you what the sermon was about when it was time to leave. My dad had his head down in his hands, and I'm not sure if he was in deep prayer or sleep. Sadly I never had a deep chat with my parents about God or Jesus. During these trips Mum never came with us; however, she surely believed in Jesus.

During the end days of my mum's life I was certain she believed in Christ, and as I was sitting at her hospital bed, I asked her flat out, "Mum, you believe in Jesus, right?"

She answered in a weak, "Uh-huh."

In my early years I went to Sunday school in church, and it was always my mum who sat with me, helping me remember the Lord's Prayer and more. She had set the wheels in motion and really got my course to find the Lord in detail going much later in my life. As the last day for her life began here on this earth, I had to drive back from Washington, DC, as a friend of hers called me to say that she looked really bad.

"You should come home as quickly as possible," the friend said. She had already been taken to the hospital, and I arrived just before she slipped away into unconsciousness.

I said, "Hi, Mum, I'm here."

She relaxed. She tried to say something, but it was not understandable. The nurse told me that there was nothing else they could do for her but try to make her as comfortable as possible and move her into a private room so I could have this last time with her. They asked if I would like someone to come and pray over her, and I said, "Yes, a priest." That was how she had grown up. The Father arrived and asked if I'd like him to give her last rites. I agreed. Here's where I'm sure she was saved. He pulled out the vial of holy oil and leaned toward her to bless her forehead. With her eyes closed and already unable to speak, even unable to squeeze my hand, she sat up, turning directly toward the priest and the holy oil. Wow! The Father was a bit taken aback by this and shared a glance with me. I just simply smiled and said to him, "She's ready to go home, Father."

You see, I believe in all of the promises of the Bible. My parents' deaths were not a time for tears. Sure, I was upset that they were not here anymore, but I knew where they were going. Really I was jealous. While I was sitting by Mum's bedside, waiting for the Lord to come and get her, I prayed, thanking Him for her. She had done all that she could do here now. "Take her home, my Lord," I said, "It's time for her to receive her reward."

This little episode with the holy oil would come back into play later in our story, as I knew this would be an answer to a prayer and the only way out of a situation that had developed (as you'll soon read).

Stepping back in time long before my parents passing on to the Lord, Sharmalie and I met up when I was twenty-four and she was a smart nineteen-year-old. We met in a bar in Georgetown, Washington, DC. I spied her from across a crowded bar. She was sitting at the bar, not talking to anybody really, which was strange, I thought, because she was beautiful. It was my lucky day! I had never had the courage to talk to women out right. It was just fate or the blessing of the Lord really that she was sharing a house with another girl who at the time happened to work in a restaurant that I was a manager of, and she actually introduced us later that evening. She likes to tell me that she actually spied me as well, sitting at the bar on top of the dance floor, and that I stuck out because there was this one spotlight that was highlighting my hair just right. She says it kind of looked like a halo. One thing led to another, and before you know it, we're married and popping out babies. Sharmalie has a special draw to her. She is British, and she has this killer accent to a Pittsburgh boy fresh out of the mills. She speaks so that you want to listen. Well, it worked on me—hook, line, and sinker. One of the best sayings I've ever heard is something some other British guy said to Sharmalie's sister, although it applies to all four of them. Read this with a British accent: "She's got eyes wot takes ducks off water." She was born in England, and she was well-traveled because her family was living in many parts of the world, the Bahamas being one of them. Her mother is pure British, and her father was Sri Lankan, an intelligent, talented civil engineer who always wore a cravat. They saw many parts of the world while she was growing up. Sharmalie came here to go to beautician school and learn to cut hair. That's when we began dating. The great thing is that I have never had to pay for a haircut in thirty years. I wonder what that works out to in savings for not ever having to pay for one. I'll bet it's a lot. Sharmalie has three younger sisters, all currently living in England, as is her mum.

Danielle is now an accomplished doctor of occupational therapy. She has two children of her own, living in the Richmond, Virginia, area. Aaron is an extraordinary wizard with computer servers and all things technical, stuff that I have difficulty understanding when he tries to tell Sharmalie and me something about his work. The kids are both products of the '80s and grew up with this stuff. When they call me and say, "Daddy, send me a text," I say okay, pick up my little post-it pad, write out a short note, put it in the envelope, and mail it! Cue the eye roll from the kids.

In the past none of us were truly saved or aware of what had to be done to be with God. We weren't bad or doing any crazy stuff that one would associate with evil. We would be considered normal by all means of the word, a normal middle-class family with middle-class problems—not enough money to meet the bills, kids getting ready for college, not attending church, but still wanting some kind of supernatural help to get all the things wrong in our lives straight. Of course Jesus wasn't about to answer that kind of prayer before He put us through trials that would move us to where He could use us. At this point in time I had started a small business that's still small today. We had overwhelming debt in credit cards (more than $40,000 from business and personal usage), two mortgages, and a growing IRS debt in excess of $80,000. (It's a long story.) It seemed no matter how much I made there was never enough, and the balances never came down.

Then the beginning to the proverbial yellow brick road to—in this case heaven—was made available. Out came the first installment of the very popular *Left Behind* series, so this is the moment our story begins—the spring of 1996 when I actually began to read the books. I didn't actually seek it out. My beautiful wife went to the local library and brought home a copy of the book in CD form. I really hate to read. I'm a listener, not a reader. If I hear it, I will remember it. If I read it, stuff usually leaks out quickly. So I started to listen and was quickly hooked.

I remember somewhere early in the series, the means to salvation were revealed. I got down on my knees and reaffirmed what I thought I had already done and gave my life to Christ. It felt good. It felt right. Only this time I prayed out loud, speaking it with my lips. Before this moment I always considered myself one of God's children, but truly I was not. One very important piece was missing. I had not prayed the prayer of salvation or the sinner's prayer with my lips, speaking my faith into existence by declaring Jesus as my Lord and Savior, asking Him to enter my life. I thought just knowing about Him and praying to Him and asking for things to be done was enough. That was a big mistake. I needed to acknowledge Him before men so that He would acknowledge me before the Father. This is when the Holy Spirit truly entered me for the first time.

Saying this prayer with your lips is important. Consider what the Bible states, "Then God said, 'Let there be light,' and there was light" (Genesis 1:3). God speaks things into existence, and therefore, so must you when you are saying and asking for eternal salvation through Jesus. The Bible says that "if you confess with your mouth the Lord Jesus and believe in your heart that God has raised Him from the dead, you will be saved. For with the heart one believes unto righteousness, and with the mouth confession is made unto salvation" (Romans 10:9–10).

Spiritually things started to heat up when I was truly saved. Up until this point I had failed my family, not being its pastor, not taking the responsibility to help save their eternal souls. It really hadn't entered into my thought process before this point; however, I'm positive that the Holy Spirit entered me at this time and began to move me onto a track that would lead me to become strong in the Word of Christ and instill a desire to teach and move my family to Him.

Demonic influences can take many forms as Jesus shows us in the Bible. I began to read the Bible, even though, as I said, reading is not my thing; however, for some reason the Bible took on a new meaning for me. I'd pick it up from time to time and read, but I really did not understand what I was reading. I wasn't gathering the meaning correctly. I thought I was, but as I grew, I learned that I had a lot to learn! I wanted to learn what the Bible really meant, but because of family pressures, I knew that church was off the radar screen for the time being. Even the mere mention to my wife of going to church was always met with a response, "You must be kidding."

This response of hers really sticks out in my mind: "I can only imagine what my sisters would say if they knew I was going to church."

Even though Sharmalie brought the book to me, at this point in time she was the furthest from God of any of us. The mere mention of God or church brought on a verbal assault, which usually led to her leaving the room or house, not wanting to deal with the subject.

Even the thought of what a family member might think served as an obstacle for us. But I always remembered this: When we take our final breath here on earth, the next person we are going to see is the Lord Jesus during judgment. He will review my life, not taking into account what anyone thought of me. It will just be me and the Lord. There won't be any lawyers to plead my case, no jury to decide my fate, just the one who knows all things. If I wanted to, I could even go through my whole life not obeying Him but thinking things were good until the moment when Jesus would look at me with burning and piercing eyes and say, "Depart from Me. I never knew you." Oh, my God, what a horrible thought. At that moment the ground would open up, and you would be separated from Him in everlasting torment, in a dark, hot place with sulfurous odor permeating everything, a sense of loss that could never be fixed, and this will be for an eternity!

So in late 1996 my interest and growth in the Word of the Lord started to take on the form of listening to our local Christian radio station, WAVA 105.1 here in the northern Virginia area. I began to listen and quickly developed a passion for some of the pastors and teachers on the programming list. From 8:00 to 11:30 a.m. with a daily diet of hearing the Word and having it explained to me, I began to quickly grow in knowledge and understanding of the Bible and the teachings of Jesus. Each of these pastors who taught the Word put it into terms that I could understand and verified its truth, showed me that it was not their meaning of the Word but that of the Lord's unyielding commandments.

My knowledge of demons and even angels for that matter at this time in my life was really lacking. This is one of the greatest tools of evil—ignorance. If you don't know and don't recognize a threat, why would you try to change it? Sitting in church and hearing about demons is completely different than your faith growing so strong that you actually try to do something to fight evil. When one is strong in faith, he or she will have the motivation to save someone.

A demon in my own home was about to make *its* presence known, turning my world into chaos. He resided in my wife and was about to change everything of value that I held dear—my family.

CHAPTER 2

First Steps to Jesus

C ommitting my life to Christ up to this point had taken from 1996 to 2007. It took more than a decade for me to grow enough in spiritual discernment to begin to recognize changes and spiritual events happening around me. As my growth in the Word and Jesus began to pick up steam, the demonic side present in my very home took notice. This stuff is really scary because it's absolutely true and real. The Devil really exists and completes his work through his angels.

I started out slowly noticing attacks at home. The radio would suddenly change stations by itself when I had WAVA on. This happened many times only when a Christian radio station was on. I began to think that this must be a spirit of a child, a practical joker. My knowledge of the demonic spirit world was too undeveloped at this time to understand the basics. The more you grow in the Spirit, the more you become aware of their presence. This certainly applies to the saved individual. I began to *feel* their presence. It was just a feeling at first—the one you get where you walk into some place and feel uncomfortable—but the more I began to know my spiritual side and pray, the more their presence became real and noticeable. I would walk around in my home and suddenly turn to an empty spot and know someone was there, even to the point of talking to it under my breath and saying, "I know what you're up to, and I'm going to fix this."

its home—I'll call this being *it* and chat more in detail about this later—was in the darkest and farthest end of our finished basement. At this time I had a computer there that I would only use for gaming. I knew *it* was there and would frequently turn around and look at that spot, terrified but still somehow resolute that the Lord would not let me down on this. His phrase kept coming to my mind. "He who is in me is greater that he who is in the world." These feelings weren't just short blips on the radar screen, the feelings of *its* presence lasted for minutes on end. Make no mistake, I was scared, not knowing how to really deal with *it*. This is one reason knowing the Bible and the Word that the Lord has given us are all of the tools necessary to defeat evil. The phrase that really stuck and the one that I began to use was commanding this spirit was, "In the name of my lord Jesus Christ, leave this house."

The only way to fight a demonic presence is to rely on Him and only Him. We have no power over these presences, but through Him this phrase can be really comforting in times of trouble and fear. But it may not be the total solution. They must obey when we bring Jesus into the situation, but they can return unless further steps are taken.

At this time I was in relative infancy as a believer, eleven years in learning so far and no pastor to learn from or to go to. I needed to search for the answers the hard way. I originally found out about using Jesus' name to command demons from my cousin Dave Terk. We would chat about stuff, and he told me about using Christ's name in defending my turf, so I began to use it. To me it was one small piece of the armor of God, which I still had no idea how to use properly. It was going to be a long road in the making, but I knew the Lord already had laid out my path. None of what happened or what was about to happen had not already been approved by our heavenly Father. The Lord was in complete control or my life. I just wasn't aware of how much at this time. I think one important part to note here is that I was actively looking to grow in the Word of the Lord, consciously doing something every day to know Him better. Please don't miss this opportunity to know Him. Read the Bible, attend church, go to Bible study, read books, or just gather with like-minded believers.

Danielle Comes to the Lord

Early in 2008 what was once simple now begins to take on a more serious battle between Sharmalie and me. At this time she was not saved, and I suspected that the one within her had begun to be aware of my change and fight back. However, the next soul to be saved belonged to my daughter, but this was done not through simple means. Evil began to pay attention to me and knew what I would do. It attacked Danielle. I'll leave it up to Danielle to explain the attack in her section; however, when we talked after the attack, Danielle was confused about what had happened and really had no idea about the spiritual attack she had just experienced. As a doctor, she chalked it up to an anxiety attack, which couldn't be further from the truth. She just didn't know it yet.

I can remember the conversation to this day years later. I was driving on our local parkway when I called her to talk about her episode several days before. At this time the Harry Potter series had started, and I actually used this to help give an analogy as an example. Danielle had an experience when she was sleeping. Something happened that woke her up and caused her to leave the house, screaming and running down the road. Demon attacks can happen in many forms. This one for Danielle was an attack in spirit. It attacked her spirit when she was asleep. She did not see or hear anything that she could remember, although it frightened her enough to leave the house screaming.

We are made up of three things—the body (our physical makeup), the soul (our thoughts and personality and our free will to choose), and the spirit (an eternal being along with our souls). Thankfully our future grandchildren were not yet born. It was just Danielle and Brian in their newly purchased house. Danielle had just experienced a spiritual attack straight out of hell not because of what she had done but because of me. She was attacked because of my conversations with Sharmalie about Danielle and bringing her to the Lord. The one within my wife was not about to let me bring my family to Jesus. This being within Sharmalie was surely aware of my strong growth in wanting to know the Lord. When the phone call started, Danielle was at work, and I was driving down the road. As I begin to explain to her what had happened, I found a side road to pull onto. I fully expected to be hit while I was driving—anything that could happen to stop me talking to her about the Lord. A quick prayer to the Lord stopped that. I then said to her, "Danielle, let me be the teacher against the dark arts for a second."

I was referring to Harry Potter, and then I told her what I thought had happened to her from a spiritual point of view. Long story short, before we ended the call, she gave her life to Christ at that time over the phone with me.

I couldn't have been happier. I thanked and praised the Lord repeatedly many times over for these blessings. Upon my arrival home I told this to Sharmalie. I will never forget what happened that night as we began to get into bed. Sharmalie was already lying in the bed as I came over and sat down on the edge of the bed. She got up on one elbow and turned to face me while she was lying there. We were not talking about anything else before I got into bed. She had this look of utter disgust on her face as though I had just done something that was unforgivable. A conversation ensued, but I knew it was not her. It was the one within her who came out fighting. During this shouting match, *it* said to me (using Sharmalie as a mouthpiece), "You're going to try to bring Aaron (our son) now, aren't you?"

"Of course," I said in a low, even, and calm voice.

it said, "Your God won't get Him. You think He's so great. You don't even know what His commandments are, do you! Do you? You can't even find them in the Bible!"

There was fire in her eyes, real anger, and when she spoke, little bits of spit flew out from her mouth, something which she would absolutely never do. Without any further word I turned and picked up the Bible off of the bedside tabletop. I hadn't looked at the Bible enough to know where the commandments really were exactly, but I think the Lord took over at this point and put me at Exodus. And without further word I began to read and speak out loud *all* of the commandments. She (and the one within) rolled over and didn't say another word. I put the Bible down and did the same.

When our Lord was tempted by the Devil in the desert, He didn't get into a verbal argument with Satan. He only said, it is written and said the Bible verse to quote God. Basically I did the same, although it also set into motion and all-out battle between He who was in me and *it* who was in my wife at the time. I knew this, and now *it* knew. Demon possessions can come in many forms, some stronger than others. In this case *it* used my wife to fulfill its desires. Sharmalie didn't hate God. *it* did, and *it* used her that way by putting words in her mouth. Look at Matthew 8:28–31.

> And when he was come to the other side into the country of the Gergesenes, there met Him two possessed with devils, coming out of the tombs, exceeding fierce, so that no man might pass by that way. And behold, they cried out saying, what have we to do with thee, Jesus, thou Son of God? Art thou come hither to torment us before the time? And there was a good way off from them an herd of many swine feeding. So the devils besought Him saying, if thou cast us out, suffer us to go into the herd of the swine.

These men were mouthing the words, but the devils (demons) were doing the speaking. There may be many reasons why some may be against God. After this episode I recognized who I was up against, and I was really upset and terrified about what to do next. (I underline against with purpose here, this word is mentioned many times in Ephesians 6:12). I had absolutely no idea, no plan, nobody I could rely on in the physical world, but what I did realize was that the Father God had just delivered one of my family to Himself. After this conversation with Sharmalie she rolled over. I lay down but did not concentrate on the fight with her, but instead I thought about the blessing that had been delivered earlier this afternoon, an answer to a prayer, my daughter's eternal salvation. How exciting!

A Comment from Danielle in Her Own Words

I have always believed in God, but I had doubts now and then as to how much this really affected my life. I am an occupational therapist and a student of science. I admit that I had my doubts about the existence of God growing up and in my adult life, but somewhere deep inside I really hoped it was true. He is much more a part of my life now than He has ever been though. I believe that my questions were slowly being answered over the course of several months, and my dad was there to explain what it all meant.

A few years back I remember reading the book *Eat, Pray, Love*. My good friend and I were reading it together, and it opened up dialogues about the existence of God or a higher power. After our discussions we came to the conclusion that it really would be great if God really was out there or in us and that He must be a loving God. The title of the book itself lends to the conclusion the author comes to. She learned to love and be loved by God. And now I remember this was January of 2008. After I finished this book, I had dream after dream that would wake me. I would feel out of sorts, but I could not remember the dream. I did, however, think that it had something to do with this book I read and all this talk about God. That is when I started having conversations with Him when I woke up or in the shower. I would ask Him if He was trying to tell me something.

One night a few weeks later in the middle of a dead sleep, I awoke with my heart beating out of my chest, and I was completely panicked! I jumped out of bed and ran down the steps of my home and out the door. I felt as if I was dying, and I was trying to run away from what was sitting on my chest. I couldn't breathe. When I returned, my husband held me on the couch all night while I tried to settle down and breathe, but I was afraid to sleep.

Several days later I was working, sitting at my desk when I had the conversation with my dad. He explained to me that I was under attack. I certainly felt as if I was out of control, unable to escape this feeling of dread. When he explained that I could be saved, give myself to Jesus, and say it out loud, I found that it just made sense to me. I felt calmed. I felt happier. It was an easy decision. In fact, I didn't really think. I just acted. I started feeling that all-consuming love and unquestionable belief that one feels as a child. I felt that I wasn't really ever going to be alone. I didn't have a good idea of what Jesus did in His lifetime or many Bible stories, but I knew that in that minute I had just introduced myself to Him.

I remember when I was younger, I used to lie in bed at night and look up at the sky. I would see the first star and make a wish. But even now as I think back to what I was wishing, it was more like a prayer every night. I would think to myself, *I should probably wish that my family and friends were happy, and then maybe what I wish for would then also come true.* I thought, *God would like that if I wished for something for someone else before myself.* I also liked going to church functions with my friends, such as choir and youth group. I even liked going to sunrise service. I thought it was so magical, everyone standing together outside to watch another day begin in the name of Jesus. I never learned that much about Jesus growing up, and I thought the story of Easter was interesting. It was a story of hope, and I liked that much more than the other bits of sermons I had heard of sin and shame. It turned me off to the services when all I wanted was to have a relationship with my simple, loving God. I even went to a church camp for several summers. In the mornings we were to go out to a single spot alone and have a chat with God or write in a journal, etc. It was nice. It was a time in my middle school and high school years when I did actually feel like it was me and God in the woods having juice together, talking about what to do about that guy who liked me or how to make one of my friends happier about her life. The answer was not God or Jesus at the time, but I am sure that He was listening.

A few years after my attacks I picked up the book *Proof of Heaven* while I was walking through the bookstore. It jumped out at me, as I was becoming more curious about God and the afterlife. The book was written by a neurosurgeon who had visited the afterlife in a near-death experience and was also compelled to write about it. I felt I was one who was meant to read this book. And Dr. Alexander wrote the book for people like me, a believer in science and someone with a compelling need for proof. After I read the book, I started picking up the Bible more often and seeing events in a more spiritual way, in a way that might have been touched by divine intervention! I was just so pulled into the description he gave of heaven. After I read the book, I feel like through his words I have also seen heaven. When I say a prayer at night, I close my eyes and imagine what he described. It's as if I am talking to God and Jesus right in their living room. It is bright and beautiful, and there is an angelic song in the background. I can say anything I want because I know I am loved unconditionally.

I also started talking to God more often and asking Jesus where He's been and what He wants me to do. So I have been attending church and have been including my husband and children. I want my children to grow up knowing and loving Jesus and to know that He loves them too. I have found through this journey so far that what I want is simple—to have a lot of *love* in my life. And I am blessed to have a loving family who will share the journey with me.

It's such a blessing to hear my daughter talk with passion about our Lord, especially after I failed so miserably in her early life to teach her what was really important and how important it is to know the Lord now before your last breath. Certainly it's a joy to read her words now and learn about how much she enjoyed sunrise services and being in church, and unfortunately I was not sharing in that part of her life.

So many families in this world are troubled by a variety of situations—relationships, drugs, or whatever is pulling your family apart—and I would like to offer this counsel. Look beyond the normal of what can be seen or heard. Look at the spiritual side of what's being said or done in your family. It is really difficult to see beyond the emotions or words of the moment; however, if you are looking for the Lord to help, see things and act upon them from His point of view. What biblical answers can relate to this situation? Place the Bible as the lead resource in your search for answers. If like most, and as I was at this point in time, understanding the Bible and discerning the correct meaning of its many points is not easy. Without a teacher to explain the proper meaning of the Word, you may be leaving many doors open for wrong interpretation.

As I said before, because Sharmalie was so against church at this time, I did not have a pastor to go to. I was basically leaderless other than listening to Christian radio. This is where a pastor or a church body can really play an important part, and you can rely on the Lord's representative on this earth (pastor) to help guide you in understanding the Bible. This person or group may lead to the correct path and possible answers for this situation. Look for as many ways as possible to grow in spiritual discernment. *Going to church one day a week won't cut it.* One will not grow enough and keep the Lord in first thought without good reinforcement continually soaking into his or her daily thoughts. On the other hand, looking for and accepting advice from someone who does not live on the biblical side of life is, I believe, even more dangerous.

This situation, as it developed in the middle of 2008, became even more apparent that I was in a battle for my family, that I had to become the Lord's warrior. I wasn't about to let Him down. He had given me the biblical responsibility to be a leader for my family and to fear no evil, wherever it was coming from, and now I was just learning how truly important and difficult this task would be. I had no idea of the real peril I was just about to be thrown into.

CHAPTER 3

Evil Can Touch the Physical World

My wife is British, and she goes home (England) at least once year or as much as we can afford it. I noticed that since my conversion to a follower of Jesus, the spiritual attacks on me were the greatest when Sharmalie was not home here in the United States. In the summer of 2008, Sharmalie headed home again. I think the attacks happened during her absences because she was not made aware of what was happening. Why would this demon want to advertise *its* existence or give value to what I might tell her? *it* meant to keep her in the dark.

I began to get to the point where every night for me was uncomfortable, and I would go to bed expecting bad stuff to happen. Most events were small, just feeling uncomfortable; however, one attack changed my view on what and how I thought evil could accomplish between the physical and spiritual worlds. We currently had two cats. Both at the time were downstairs. While I was asleep and face down in the bed, I awoke abruptly, did a push-up, looked into the bed, and screamed at the top of my lungs, *"No!"* As I became more aware, I thought about how this scream was really weird, and I couldn't pin it to anything in particular. Then I turned over onto my back. I lay in the bed with a small night-light on. (All these feelings made me aware and not comfortable in the dark just as a little child.) It was summertime, so I didn't have any sheets on, and I slept in the nude. This is when the most terrifying thing happened to me that I hope cannot be repeated. I looked down at my right leg. Something was squeezing my right leg from underneath and through the bed, pinning my leg down. It felt as though many hands were grabbing my thigh and shin areas at the same time, making pulsing finger indentations in my leg. These were *visible* to me, and I could *feel* them as well. I did not see what was grabbing me, just the indentations pulsing on my leg. This really terrified me. I know I tried to say, "In the name of my Lord Jesus Christ I command you to leave this house."

But I think it only came out as a garbled mess. Luckily it seemed to work because the invisible hands stopped. In retrospect I began to realize that I could not speak the words clearly during this time because my lips were being held tightly shut to keep me from saying the words to command evil to go. I got up, turned on every light I could, and grabbed the Bible off the bedside table. I took the Bible with me, which gave me a sense of security. I went downstairs to lie down on the couch. Both of our cats must have sensed something because they came into the living room. Milo got on my stomach, and Jeeves, the older of the two, lay at the base of the couch next to me. I never felt so good to have somebody with me, even if they were just cats. The rest of the night was uneventful. I lay there, praying, asking the Lord to intercede on my behalf.

There was no denying the battle I was now engaged in. Not only was it involving me, but as I feared it would also involve all whom I loved. What makes a man, a father, and a husband stand up and offer himself as a target when all that he loves is threatened? How can he fight something he cannot see, has no control over personally, or cannot dictate the course of actions to correct either? This is what I was thinking at the time, and of course, I was all wrong. I had all of the answers. They were in the Bible, at church, holy oil, and have faith in He who is in me, I just needed to fight this battle on my knees in prayer. This situation brought that fact into the light.

After this episode I no longer began sleeping with the Bible on the bedside table. It moved to a new location on top of the pillow next to me. I started to go to bed with the Bible in my hand just in case, and what a comfort it added to my very being, knowing the Word was with me literally in my hands at the ready for me to use.

Just as evil reached out and touched me here, so had good. At a later period of time again when I was completely asleep in bed, Sharmalie lying next to me, I was suddenly moved to wake up because someone was holding my right hand, just a gentle but firm hand holding mine. I was then completely awake. I looked into my headboard, staring forward at this invisible force while my hand was being held. Wow, I knew this experience was for real, and I wanted to tell Sharmalie. As soon as I whispered her name to tell her what was going on, the force let go of my hand, and I no longer felt anything. There were no feelings of dread or fright on my behalf, so I marked this up to an angel being sent by God to tell me He was here with me in my struggles.

Again I'd like to restate what the Bible says. "For we do not wrestle against flesh and blood, but against principalities, against powers, against the rulers of darkness of this age, against spiritual hosts of wickedness in heavenly places" (Ephesians 6:12).

CHAPTER 4

Family Challenges and Rewards

I t was now the winter of 2009. I kept an open heart that the Lord would answer my prayers that my family would come to Him. He answered that prayer in a way that was totally unexpected, not in one big open change but in a small number of changes that helped bring my final two members of my family to Him. Sharmalie, Aaron, and I went to England for a vacation during Christmas holiday. We were with Sharmalie's family during this time, and my son, Aaron, gave me the best Christmas present I could have ever received. It was Christmas Eve, and Sharmalie was supposed to go out with some of her school friends that night for a short time, which would leave Aaron and I to keep ourselves entertained, so we agreed to walk up to the nearest pub, which was about one mile away from the house, and have a beer as Daddy and son. As it turned out, I think we got there at about 5:00 p.m., and it was fairly busy. We ordered a pint each and sat down by the fireplace. Somehow the conversation turned toward the Lord, and for the next three hours everyone else in this busy pub disappeared to us. We chatted solely about the Lord and His Word. I did most of the talking, and Aaron really listened and took it in. He asked thoughtful questions, and we discussed them. When we realized the time, we called our chat over, got up, and went back to the house. During the whole walk back home on this beautiful snowy walk, I was looking up and praising the Lord for allowing me to talk to my son about Him. What a Christmas present! Aaron did not come to the Lord yet. He just wasn't there yet, but the mustard seed had been planted.

Then the next day after Christmas dinner, both Aaron and Sharmalie were secretly thinking of the Lord. They just didn't make it known to me at the time. I had no idea the Holy Spirit was already working on her. Both saw an attack happen on me by one of her sisters. They just didn't realize it until we chatted about it later. While nearly the whole family was sitting around the kitchen table, my sister-in law out of the blue asked me, "Do you really believe in Jesus?" As she asked this question of me, but directed her gaze toward Sharmalie, which I viewed as an attempt by the one within to have Sharmalie verbally deny Christ. She did not.

My answer came out garbled from the abrupt and blunt query, and I said, "One thousand percent."

No one else around the table followed up the question. I was ready to continue the debate, but something told me, "Not now," so I let it go from there. To date, as far as Sharmalie and I are aware, the British side of our family have yet to come to Christ. We pray that changes. So at the time of this event around the table, I was the only believer in Christ in a room of ten people. I'm sure that this opportunity will present itself again, but this time there will be at least two believers in the room, Sharmalie and me, for the Lord says that "when two or more gather in My name, I will be there." That will be the time to address them and those within.

The experience with Sharmalie's family was uncomfortable, but I've learned that I'm not the only person who has experienced family difficulties. Sometimes no matter what you do, you don't feel like progress is being made. Where should you go to first for an answer? A friend? Another family member? Think about which way to attack an issue. I'd like to offer this counsel, one that I am sure that works. First go to God! Our heavenly Father wants all to come to Him just as you would wish your sons or daughters would always come to you with their problems. We live in a world of instant gratification. We look for quick answers for everything. Many times the Lord does not work that way. Have faith that you are heard. Our problems exist in many cases because we choose to see or solve them through worldly means without relying on Him. Think in His terms. Think beyond the visible and look into the spirit world, where Jesus is the King of Kings. Hear the Word of our Lord, "And whatever you do in word or deed, do all in the name of The Lord Jesus, giving thanks to God the Father through Him" (Colossians 3:17). That sets your priority. Go to Jesus first. How can He create man, the world, and the universe and not be able to handle a prayer from you?

He is capable. Later Jesus would come to me through a vision, answering prayers that I had. I can say that your prayers *will* be heard if covered by the blood of Christ. If not, then come to Him. Our Lord said, "Whoever calls on My name shall be saved."

He will hear you then. Trust this! I would like to suggest that you be careful here. There are folks who say "that God told them." That's all well and fine if you can discern it is His voice and the will of God from your own. Be careful not to infuse thoughts, believing an answer from God has been given. Ask yourself, "Is this something Jesus would do or say? Is this within the will of God as stated in the scripture of the Bible?" When unsure, go to the Bible and go to your pastor.

Remember that Our Lord is listening to your prayer or calling on Him. I visualize talking to God like this: Think of the old-time phones, the ones where a person would pick up a cumbersome handset, which is basically an oversized ear and mouthpiece. The mouthpiece is where prayer goes in and you call God for an answer. The earpiece is the receiver, and you're waiting to hear His reply. This is the faith end of the phone. How long are you willing to stay on the line for an answer? If faith and patience are not sincere or steadfast, you may hang up before you receive the answer. Later in the book I will review a vision that was given to me by the Lord, and I realized that I did just that. I hung up before I got all of the answer that I thought I needed, which was being shown by the Holy Spirit for a reason.

CHAPTER 5

it

I called the one within my wife *it* because I cannot explain this being any better or give *it* any value with a name. Even when I am referring to *it*, *it* will be written in no capitalized letters, not even if starting out a sentence. I'm sure this will make all of the English teachers cringe. I am drawing attention to *it* with italicized letters and an underlined style not to give a special call out to *it* but just to make clear when I'm talking about this evil entity. This creature would make *its* presence known again at home in our bedroom after we returned from our England trip in the winter of 2009. Things were changing inside Sharmalie, and *it* knew this. Stuff was going to start happening rapidly now as it tried to regain control of her. *it* was going to lie about all that was true in our relationship and in the Bible.

Sharmalie and I were both upstairs. As we were trading places in the bathroom, a mild argument began, and I accused her of something. Jealousy is a powerful tool used by evil to place obstacles in the path of a loving couple. It can manufacture things that just are not true. Both parties will know this, but we ignored the facts and concentrated on the fear that *it* was putting in place between us. Sharmalie was facing an open closet, and during the argument as I began to walk past her from behind, her back to me, I saw her face looking at me as I passed by. And *it* said using Sharmalie's own voice to my ear, "What does that matter?"

I continued walking to the bed, which was a short distance away, maybe about five seconds, enough time to ask myself, "Did I really just see that?" I turned to her and said, "What do you mean what does that matter?"

Sharmalie then turned to me and said, "What are you talking about? I didn't say that!"

I didn't answer because I quickly realized what had just happened. I didn't bring this up to her because at this point in time *it* was in control of her inner thoughts. She was completely unaware of what was happening to her, kind of like what happened to my mother in the latter stages of her life. She had a cancerous brain tumor that slowly wiped out all awareness of everything to her left in her line of vision; however, she was not aware of this. When a demon controls the inner soul, it can be transparent to the affected individual but known to someone the Holy Spirit controls, someone who is aware of spiritual things. The Bible tells us to put on the whole armor of God. Without the whole package, you can be open to attacks. The Devil has had a long time to learn his craft. He will do everything in his power to ruin your relationship with the Lord.

This is the second time *it* manifested itself to me. The first time was when *it* physically grabbed me from under and through the bed, and *it* obviously was talking to me because I awoke and shouted. "No!" However, I do not remember anything said. Now *it* chose to show me directly by sight. I did not see a demon looking all ugly and stuff like the movies. *It* chose to talk to me by using my wife's voice and her face. These demons are the real deal. They really do exist. I never watch spooky movies. Think zombies are cool? Even a basic review of the book of Revelation tells us that for a time during this period many will wish to die but death will not come. I would like to suggest that at this time many may look just like that. I don't believe that any true Christian that fears the Lord and knows and believes the Bible could ever watch or support some of the junk that we see thrown on TV and the movies today. They just have no idea what's coming and certainly are not looking at life through spiritual eyes. *When one starts to experience this stuff for real, one has no appetite to hang around in their world.*

It was also in these early years during conversations with Sharmalie that she told me that she had been hearing little voices inside her head. She commented that she could never understand what they were saying, but she knew they were definitely there. They weren't always heard, just sometimes. I never really made the connection that these voices could represent something more. I still had not grown strong enough in faith or knowledge of the Word to put two and two together and see the true spiritual nature behind this.

I was in full-fledged spiritual warfare. _it_ was no longer worried about hiding _its_ true intentions. When I lay down at night, my conscious mind was fearful, but the Holy Spirit was strong. God controlled my spirit, so what was I to fear? Here's where the power of the Holy Spirit takes command over evil. My thoughts went immediately to Jesus praying in the garden of Gethsemane, where our Lord said, "Watch and pray, lest you enter into temptation. The spirit indeed is willing, but the flesh is weak" (Matthew 26:41).

The Lord had already won this fight over evil at the cross, and He was in me, so by Him I had already defeated this evil in my home. It was a work in progress, not the Lord's battle against evil but my growth of faith in Him that I might become strong enough to fight evil, be it in thought or deed. Iron was sharpening iron.

CHAPTER 6

Something Completely Unexpected

In January 2010, we were having another argument, but this one was different. It was very possibly a marriage-ending argument. Once more *it* would use jealousy as a tool to come between us. Our major arguments almost always dealt with this. Money was never really an issue because we never had it. You couldn't argue over something you don't have, and neither of us never really cared too much to have more. It's strange how money never has been the fault of an argument between us. I was completely ready, depending on the answers I received from Sharmalie, to end our time together as a couple and a family. The one thing that meant the most to me in the world was about to end. I knew it, and so did she. During the process she wanted to run and not discuss our issues. She finally agreed to come and sit back down. In tears, she said out of the blue, "That's why I took us to St. Paul's Cathedral in London. I thought something would happen there for me if it was going to happen at all."

That statement completely stopped me in my tracks. I said, "You're looking to be saved?"

She said, "Didn't I just say that?" The value that I place on my family is second only to the Lord, and here He was opening the door for her to come in.

I said to her, "If He can forgive you, then so can I."

I got down on my knees in front of her, grabbed her hands, looked into her eyes, and said to her, "Repeat this prayer after me. Say it with your lips and mean it in your heart, and the Holy Spirit will come in.

Remarkably *it* tried to manage this one last time by making Sharmalie say, "Can't I just think it?"

I told her and this being possessing her, "No, you must say this with your lips and mean it in your heart. Babe, repeat after me. Lord Jesus, I believe You came into this world and died for my sins. I ask You to come into my heart and soul. I receive You as my Lord and Savior."

Once she said this, we both got on our knees on the hard tile floor, and I prayed the most well-meaning prayer of thanks that I could muster directly from the heart. The Lord had brought my wife, whom I believed would not come to Him, straight through the narrow door, a door that Christ Himself said was narrow. That was two down with one more to go!

Wow, things had really taken a turn in our lives. I knew I was no longer sleeping with the enemy. My wife was now with the Lord, and the Holy Spirit was in control. I now had someone to share Him with and grow with me. To this day I am completely floored at how the Holy Spirit is working through her. She is completely changed and hungers for the Word of the Bible as much as I do. Now not only do I have someone sharing my life in complete harmony with me, but we also recognize that we will know each other for an eternity. What a glorious thought. Before, I couldn't even mention going to church or bring God up in a conversation. Now we attend a local church (which was Sharmalie's idea). We listen together to Dr. David Jerimiah every day or night on the radio or computer. When we first started going to church together, Sharmalie would cry during the service for about the first month. (In our story this happens later, but I thought I would give you a taste of this now.) I just reassured her that the Holy Spirit was truly residing in her and convicting her of her faith in the Lord! Oh, give thanks to the Lord, for He is good!

Remember that I prayed for this to happen for years before the Lord actually answered this prayer and brought Sharmalie into His grace. He did it in the best fashion possible. It really meant something at the time that it happened. Are you in a marriage where one is saved and the other is not? That's difficult to acknowledge and even tougher to deal with. Before Sharmalie came to the Lord, I felt empty, even though we were in a marriage. I believe others may feel this as well, but they may not know how to handle it. Some have extramarital affairs but don't really know why or what they are looking for, and they are never fulfilled. For me I became a warrior for the Lord. I put my effort with Him in the lead, my prayer life, listening to Christian radio. I just chose to seek an answer through Christ. That was the best possible outcome. Why? Because I already had a woman who was the mother of our children, a beautiful, smart, perfect mummy. The only thing missing in our lives was the Lord, which changed through prayers to God so that He let Sharmalie hear His calling.

Our love has grown exponentially since she came to the Lord. Sharmalie's life has changed drastically as well. She now goes to Bible study, meeting many other women who also love the Lord, and they share studies of the Bible, experiences of home life, and many testimonies about how they came to know the Lord. One of the telling factors in knowing that you are truly saved is how you have changed since the Holy Spirit entered your life. In Sharmalie's case it's been dramatic. Before she came to Jesus, Sharmalie was very interested in following horoscopes and occasionally visiting with psychics, workers of iniquities who dole out false beliefs. That urge or interest is completely gone. I love her so much today. I smile broadly when she is not looking at me, watching her at church or going to these Bible studies. What a true gift from the Lord. To the reader who is experiencing these kind of challenges at home, be persistent in your prayer. When I feel I need a special prayer to make it to the Father's ears, I add this to the end of my prayer: "Holy Spirit, please carry this prayer to the Father's ears so that

He may hear." I believe putting it that way and using the terminology of the Bible adds power to your prayer.

Sharmalie and I were just driving around one night while I had to work all night long doing snow removal, and out of the blue she says, "Did you know that *devil* spelled backwards is *lived*? I wonder what the significance of that is." I immediately thought of this. The Devil was a living creature while he was in heaven under God, but when he was removed because he wanted to be like the Most High, he died just as God told Adam and Eve that they would surely die if they ate of the forbidden fruit. See the parallel there? So using the past tense of the word *lived* is correct. He once was alive but is now dead in God! Then Sharmalie came out with this little nugget: "Did you know that spelling *live* backward is *evil*?" Surely this must represent the constant battle between good and evil. One is to live, and the other is to die. I'm sure someone else has already come up with this, but we had not seen this before and just wanted to make note of it here. The Holy Spirit was making such an impact on her life that she started actively looking items up on her smartphone in relation to Jesus. Wow, what an impact the Spirit has!

A very short time after Sharmalie began to call Jesus her Lord and Savior, she was given her first message from the Lord. We had met Knox and Bev Swayze (our current copastors) and knew that they and were pastors of a church in our area, but we were not yet attending any church. We awoke one morning, and Sharmalie told me that she had had a strange dream last night.

"Oh yeah, what about?" I said.

"Knox was saying to me over and over John 3:16. What is the Bible verse that is John 3:16?"

At the time I didn't even know for sure, so I said, "Let's go look it up."

It's fantastic how the Lord works, isn't it?

Sharmalie had a burning question on her heart after she said the prayer of salvation and asked, "How do you know that it took? That you're really saved?"

I didn't have to try to really define that for her. Jesus answered her in a dream. The Bible states, "For God so loved the world that he gave his only begotten son, that whomever believes in Him should not perish but have everlasting life. For God did not send his son into the world to condemn the world, but that the world through Him might be saved" (John 3:16–17).

Yes, we can actually bring someone to Christ. This is our responsibility. Christ commanded us to love one another, be that person in your family or outside of the immediate family. People should feel they want the best for others and be willing to tell them about Christ. Once you begin to step out to proclaim Christ, now you become a threat to the Prince of the Air (the Devil), and he will begin to take notice. The Bible says, "Wherein in time past ye walked according to the course of this world, according to the prince of the power of the air, the spirit that now worketh in the children of disobedience" (Ephesians 2:2). Being truly spiritually aware and ready means situations have a different tone because you know that what someone says may not be of their own accord but coming from somewhere evil. Certainly this is the case when you're talking to unbelievers. This is nothing to fear, for the Bible states, "You are of God, little children, and have overcome them, because He who is in you is greater than he who is in the world" (John 4:4).

Many are afraid to talk to unbelievers about Christ, to uphold their faith in Him. However, think of a situation like this: If you are being attacked by someone in a dark alley, you know you're going to get hurt. If Jesus is standing there beside you, He can surely defend you, but He says, "I don't want to get involved. I'm just not feeling up to it today. You handle it." Obviously that would never come out of the mouth of our Lord, but does it come out of ours when it's time to defend Him or talk to an unbeliever about Him? Sure it has. We all have failed Him, but He has not failed us. Even before the beginning of time He knew you. He became the Son of Man for us and gave the last full measure of His humanity for us. What do you have, and what are you willing to give to Him? He asks for nothing but that you believe in Him and call Him Lord and Savior and that you love and worship Him by keeping God's commandments. John 15:5 says, "I am the vine, ye are the branches: He that abideth in me, and I in Him, the same bringth forth much fruit: for without me ye can do nothing."

How many times has the rooster crowed in your walk with the Lord? If you're like me, then many. We as man and woman constantly fail the Lord through sin or denial of our faith by failing to uphold our faith when challenged. The Apostle Peter's three denials of the Lord was meant to teach us all that we are open to these attacks from Satan. Luke 22:31–34 says,

> And The Lord said, Simon, Simon, behold, Satan hath desired to have you, that he may sift you as wheat: but I have prayed for thee, that thy faith fail not; and when thou art converted, strengthen thy brethren. And he said unto Him, Lord, I am ready to go with thee, both into prison, and to death. And he said, I tell thee, Peter, the cock shall not crow this day, before thou shalt thrice deny that thou knowest me.

Many opportunities will present themselves to promote and/or support our Lord. The strength of your faith will be tested. Have courage that He is beside you and will not fail. I believe that when the time is right, the words will be given. Moses saw himself as too weak and without the right words. He asked, "Who am I that I should do these things?"

The Lord told him, "I am with you and will give you the words in that time."

Do you think we are any less worthy than Moses? We are not in the eyes of the Lord. He loves us all and will not lose any whom the Father has given Him. When you are confronting unbelievers, just remember that it's not up to us if they actually come to Christ or not. That's up to the Lord. We are an important tool that will plant the mustard seed that He will use to help them understand and make that decision themselves. Strive to not become the branch that does not bear any fruit.

A Comment from Sharmalie in Her Own Words

Where do I begin to tell the story of how great a love can be? The sweet love story that is older than the sea—

Do you recognize the lyrics from the film *Love Story*?

Look up the lyrics; they express how I feel about God. I grew up in Essex mostly, although I lived in Sri Lanka and Jamaica and the Bahamas until I settled in America. I did not have a formal religious education. In the 1960s and '70s in England, though, we still said prayers in school, sang hymns, said grace, and I had RE (religious education) in secondary school. So I heard the Bible stories, but they were just lovely stories. It was never made clear to me that I had to accept that God gave His only Son for us and that I had to repent in order to be saved. It has taken a long time really for me to come to that realization, and how I've changed! I don't know if it is obvious to anyone else, but the peace I have and assurance that I have God to depend on forever is amazing!

I wish that I could have had this when Daddy was still alive. I know that he was a practicing Christian and asked me about going to church when he was here for Danielle's wedding. Still at least I know I'll see him again. I have so much to catch up on. I am going to Bible study and church. (I never thought in a million years I would do that!) And what an amazing group of people we have met—fun, interesting, loving, generous, intelligent people, not a bunch of fuddy-duddies who never have any fun and judge you. That sadly is the impression I had always had. From where I don't know! I couldn't have been more wrong about that. These charming people are so full of love and joy. It just beams out of them. I hope that people can see that in me because that is how I feel.

Now both of my beautiful children are saved and of course my gorgeous husband. Now I just need to persuade my family, who are all over the world, what a beautiful state it is to be in, to know how loved you are by God, to feel secure and to not worry about things beyond our control and understanding. He's got a plan for us all, His children, and all we have to do is trust and believe in Him. And then we will be taken care of. Now that is a hard thing to do—to just give it over to

God. I am still learning to let it go, but it gets easier. The more I read the Bible, the more amazed I am of the love he has for us. I still have so many questions, and some of them may never be answered. But I have faith, and yes, faith is enough for me.

CHAPTER 7

Financial Mess

The Lord didn't put my family in the financial mess I'm about to share with the world here. I succeeded in screwing this all up on my own because I didn't know enough of the Bible and remember Jesus' comments on how to handle money. If I did know, I chose to ignore the Bible and got us into tons of hot water. We had so much debt I felt like I could not even see the surface of this deep pool I dropped my family into.

I'm not sure, but I think that when the evil spirits lose one they had controlled before, they must pay a terrible price to their master, the Devil, because *it* didn't give up on creating hardship or pain in our lives. Debt was still very high, and we would get hit with something new all of the time, putting additional strain on a financial budget, but being in the Lord, knowing quite sure that He would answer prayers, these roadblocks supplied by evil didn't affect us the way they might have had we not been in Him.

Sharmalie had a nagging hip problem that was finally diagnosed as advanced arthritis in her hip, and it was recommended that the hip joint be replaced. At the time we had no insurance, so I signed up for some that might do the trick, trying to hold off doing the surgery long enough so we could be sure that they would pay for it. We didn't make it. The surgery took place in January 2012, and we were in the plan only for five months. I knew that the Holy Spirit was with her though. When she was recovering from surgery, I spent the first night with her at her side in the hospital room. Sharmalie turned to me and asked me to pray over her. *Wow!* I happily agreed and prayed with her. Then I lowered myself into bed and quietly cried while I prayed for the numerous blessings the Lord had given me!

When we were going through the deepest part of this financial mess, I would go to bed at night and pray to our Lord, saying, "Lord, I'm not as strong as Job. I can't handle this. I lay it all at Your feet, Lord."

I had to lay the bills out on the floor because there was not enough desk space to put all of them. I'm not joking here. Many were second or third notices of nonpayment. Although something always turned up and I paid the debt off or down, I was under no illusion that I could do so because of something I did. It was an answered prayer. Give praise to our Lord.

At the time we were in the midst of this part of our trials, I'm sure I could have been diagnosed with depression. I remember the point that I realized this. A couple of months after the surgery in March of 2012, Sharmalie was again in England, and I was watching TV at home. I had just gone out to bring the mail in. There were two large envelopes from our insurance company, and I was sure that these were the results of the bills for Sharmalie's hospital visit. I threw them onto the table, not wanting to look at them, and went back to watching TV. But I couldn't concentrate. I knew they were there waiting and weren't going to go away. A commercial came on about vacationing in the Caribbean, and I thought. *Well, there's something I'll never be able to afford and see*, and I began to cry like a toddler. The tears were pouring out, and I just could not stop. I remember thinking, *Oh no, I'm in depression.* However, my thoughts went immediately to the Lord and cried out to Him, blessing His ways with me. I stopped crying. I tried to make it over to the envelopes, but I didn't make it. I got down on my knees and began crying hard again, really sobbing hard. I remember saying to the Lord, "If I could only be allowed to touch the corner of your robe, I would be made whole again."

After I composed myself, I found enough courage to make it over to the insurance envelopes and began to open the biggest of the packets. I was sure I would find bad news about them covering the hospital and doctor expenses.

The Lord was already way ahead of me. He had answered my first prayer to have the insurance cover the expenses. I read the cover letter, and it explained what expenses they had covered. It was not great coverage, but it was something. We still had to come up with $13,000, and that's just covering the hospital expense. The doctors' bills were rolling in separately, but to me that was an answer to my prayers. I prayed for help on this so many times, not sure if I deserved His attention. It was almost a hope that He would not let me fight through this mess by myself. This is where His grace was offered. I had not yet begun to give money to the church and to plant the financial seed for a financial blessing. That was to come later; however, in the Lord's unyielding love for His creation, He chose to answer this prayer now by His grace and not my need. In other words, He gave me something I didn't deserve. There's no way we had anywhere close to that amount of money, but I knew I had the Lord's ear. How great is that.

So many folks have been hurt in today's economy. How is it possible to make anyone feel better after they have lost a home, when bill collectors are calling daily for payments that cannot be met? Here's where being a Christian can set you apart from the masses. Support your church either in financial blessings or with you time and talents. Extend help to those who suffer in silence. Some you know, and some you don't. Do you walk by folks on the street who ask for handouts and do not feel guilty about it? The Bible says, "And the king will answer and say to them, Assuredly, I say to you, inasmuch as you did it to one of the least of these my brethren, you did it to me" (Matthew 25:40). The Holy Spirit will use us in many ways. He may be letting us know when we are missing an opportunity to do the Lord's work by that little or great guilty feeling when we fail to show up at the plate after we are given the opportunity to help.

Think of the book of Job here. Here's a guy that had everything and then lost everything with the permission of God. The Bible states the Lord said to Satan, "Behold, all that he has is in your power; only do not lay hand on his person" (Job 1:12). Satan took all of his possessions, including the lives of his children, yet the Bible also states, "In all this Job did not sin nor charge god with wrong" (Job 1:22). Think of what this has taught to generations of folks who came after him reading his story in the Bible. His story is not that much different to many today, although what is striking is how Job handled his test of faith compared to how each of us handle these challenges of faith today.

Don't let the world's problems get in the way of your walk with God. Keep your eyes on Him and walk with Him in His blessings as He sees they should be delivered. I want to stress here that the Lord hears you. I can say that easily without hesitation. If you know Him and now call Him Lord and Savior, your prayers are heard and answered in His will and time. Our Lord knows the past, present, and future. Remember he is I Am. He always has been and always will be. "I am the Alpha and the Omega," says the Lord.

CHAPTER 8

Jesus Comes to Me in a Vision

We were lying in bed, and both of us were asleep. Suddenly I became fully aware but physically still asleep. Again as John said, "Immediately I was in spirit." This was happening to me. I was fully aware but still asleep. I was standing next to what I viewed as a bench, looking at a man who was sitting. I was standing to His left side. He was looking down at His knees with His hands folded in front of Him. My whole view of Him was not obstructed, and I was aware of nothing else around Him. Very clearly I hear Him say, "Do you believe in Jesus Christ?"

I heard myself answer, "Yes, I do."

But my answer did not come from where I was standing. My voice seemed to come from slightly above and to the left of me. The next thing I knew I was focused on the face of this man at a forty-five-degree angle, looking directly at His face from a distance of about eighteen inches. There was no expression on His face, and He continued looking straight forward. This lasted for about five seconds. Then I was placed directly in front of Him, looking directly into His eyes. He was looking back at me with no expression from Him and none from me, and as far as I could tell, I was in control of none of this, not even my own placement. Then I found myself standing where I had started. He began to lean and turn toward me. As He did, He looked at me and smiled, and I felt this power and a need to protect myself. I raised my right arm up with my fist closed. He quickly came toward me and covered my hand and then all of me. Then all of my vision went black, but I was still very aware. Then the most remarkable thing happened. I very clearly heard Him say, "Now breathe."

As He said this, it seemed as though it was coming from everywhere, all around me, and finally the vision ended. When I awoke, I had this very strong feeling. He was a really good-looking guy! Wow, that was strange! If The Lord would walk in front of me today, I probably couldn't pick Him out from the vision. I don't believe I was meant to, but what I can remember ringing in my ears is His voice. It came from everywhere. In fact, there are many nights when we first lay down in bed, I'll review this with Sharmalie again, trying to tune my voice to the Lord's so that Sharmalie can hear what He sounded like. Sometime afterward, even up until today, I keep thinking of this phrase that says, "My sheep know My voice."

He looked to me the way many of the pictures portray Christ today, but what I came away with was an overwhelming feeling that He's a really good-looking guy. His voice was powerful, not quite as deep as James Earl Jones and was very rich in tone.

Upon reviewing the vision my understanding about what really happen comes to this: The first thing Jesus asked me in a conversational tone was, "Do you believe in Jesus Christ?" He asked this the way you might ask the kids, "What do you want for dinner?" He wasn't asking it because He needed to know. He knows all. The question was for me to confirm what I knew to be true, and the answer that I gave was for me. I said, "Yes, I do." The next thing He said to me was a commandment, "Now breathe." The tone of His voice and the way He said it all point to me not having a choice. When I remember this moment, it still gives me chills to know that I have heard the Lord issue the first command ever said to man in the garden during creation as He formed a lump of dirt into man and breathed life into it to make Adam. Wow!

Why did He come? Why to me? I can only answer this because of the trials my family and I have endured to move us into a position where He can use us. I have prayed often for my trials to be over. I view it as an answer to this prayer. I also believe that the Lord has imparted some knowledge to me about what's to come for all of us. When He comes again for the church and calls us up to meet Him in the clouds during the rapture (the first day of forever), we will receive our eternal bodies and be created new in Him. At that time I think (though nothing in the Bible says this) that He will say to all of us, "Now breathe," and we will begin our new lives in Him as citizens of heaven. I can't wait!

The Plan

After the experience with the Lord, this really spurred me on to get our lives straight in the eyes of our Lord. Too many things in our lives were not in keeping with His Word and commandments. It was time to fix that. As the man and pastor/teacher responsible for my family, I took the lead in prayer, asking the Lord to show me what needed to be corrected, and He laid items on my heart that I knew needed attention. The plan that I developed had these three steps:

1. Make our home a safe place protected from evil presences.
2. Consummate our marriage in the eyes of God.
3. Make church an important part of our lives.

First I needed to take care of the fact that we did not have a safe place away from evil. The house, the car, and the plane needed to be blessed by using holy oil. Then they would be protected from evil influence. Secondly, for more than thirty years, Sharmalie and I had been in a marriage under man's law but not under God's. We had never been married by a pastor, only a justice of the peace. Therefore, in God's eyes we weren't in a proper union. I got down on one knee in our kitchen, and I asked Sharmalie to marry me again. Luckily she said, "If you insist."

I said, "I insist."

I had already arranged the marriage with a friend of ours Darrell Bailey, who had become a minister, and he agreed to perform the ceremony. Thirdly we had to begin going to church, tithing to the Lord's house and the church's needs, I could give as much money as possible, aiming for the 10 percent level, but I could also give the gifts He has blessed me with, which up until now had not been given back to honor Him. That was to change.

I would like to take this opportunity to challenge all of my brothers and sisters in Christ to develop their own plans to get right with God. Most who work in business are familiar with making business plans of all sorts and being measured on how well objectives are accomplished against these plans. Just take this step for your family's walk with Christ. I believe this is far more important than any plan you'll ever make. As a husband or the man of the family, this is your responsibility. You cannot delegate this. Jesus will hold men responsible for the family, as it was in the beginning with Adam and Eve. By making the plan and committing the thoughts and actions to paper, you increase the chances of completing the plan with excellent results. This will sound familiar to those in business. God will hold the man responsible at judgment. There will not be time to take corrective action then. That time will have passed. There will only be time for the review. I want to be in the position at that time to hear my Lord say, "Well done, good and faithful servant."

I'm not looking to get fired in actions or in hell.

My plan was pretty short. Yours may not be. It's up to you and the Lord. The important part, however, was that I now knew what I was going to do, and I began to focus my efforts with all of my family's knowledge on what was to be done. Just as in business or sports, we needed to work as a team to accomplish this goal as a team. Most of this began to happen when my daughter and wife were saved. Aaron had yet to come to the Lord, although he was putting up no resistance to what I was doing. On the other hand, he was not doing anything outright to support it either. What is important to note is that he was watching, learning, and beginning to be inspired by the Holy Spirit to come to Jesus. The Lord was already calling Aaron. He just had to open the door and let Him in.

The plan forced me to focus, and at this time I began to become an immovable object for the Lord. Many obstacles would arise and would try to move me from accomplishing what I believe the Lord laid on my heart. I had never been so focused on anything before. Daily I would be acting on the plan to move us as a family closer to completing our goals. Of course when demons come calling in your life for real, it's easy to become motivated.

My plan was based on what I knew God wanted from my family. But I know that not all readers will have husbands who can lead the family in Christ's Word. To my sisters in Christ, challenge your husband to lead the family in Christ's Word. Use this book if you feel it will help. It will be much harder for those with husbands who are not saved by Christ. Make prayer a priority in your daily life. Pray that the Lord move your husband into the light. I had to do this for years before Sharmalie came, but if it's in His will, this will happen. There are many women of the Bible, all of whom were important in moving men to positions where God could use them. You can and will have this effect on your man as well. It's your biblical responsibility to support and help him move into the correct position to accept the Lord. You *can* do this. It takes faith and belief in Jesus that He will answer this prayer. You can influence a man in many more ways than you are aware of. Read the Bible again and concentrate on all of the stories about women and see what the Holy Spirit reveals. I believe you will be motivated anew.

Chapter 9

it Reaches Out Again, and This Time the Lord Reacts

S o with the plan set, it was time to start, but before I could get a head of steam up, *it* showed up again—this time showing me *its* anger and doing things I did not believe or know were possible. We were lying in bed and close to falling asleep when I heard this great rush of wind come by my ear. It startled me. I couldn't figure out what it was. It was certainly not anywhere else in the room. I could tell it happened near me. Immediately I got excited. I thought it was our Lord coming back again and woke Sharmalie and said, "Babe, he's here again."

Half asleep, she said, "Who?"

I said, "The Lord. He's come back."

Sharmalie really didn't pay attention to me at this time. She just rolled over and continued to go back to sleep. With eyes wide open, I listened expectantly. Then I received what I can best describe as a gut punch. It was hard enough to make me double over, and I made the same sound as if one were punched. What was that? I was expecting the

Lord, and I get punched? It didn't take long to put this in the proper light. *it* was here again. Nothing felt right or good. This time I was not scared but angry. I commanded *it* to go in Jesus' name.

I believe the Lord allowed these incidents to take place to sharpen the iron, to get me ready for how He intends to use me. A few months later something truly remarkable happened. I went to bed early, and Sharmalie remained downstairs reading. As I was about to fall into bed, I said a quick prayer, "Oh, Lord, please let me be in the generation that gets raptured."

Almost asleep, lying on my right side, I become aware of a strong force pushing my right leg down into the bed and felt as though the five fingers were easily felt. Then a strong pain in my stomach ensued, doubling me over while I was lying in the bed. I thought that I was clearly calling out Sharmalie's name. Then the pain ended, and Sharmalie came running into the room.

She asked, "What's wrong? You were moaning."

I said, "No, I wasn't. I was clearly calling out your name." I began to tell her what had just happened.

She said, "What was it?" But I didn't know. I seemed fine, so she left the room to go back downstairs to read.

I got up and went into the bathroom to relieve myself. As I was looking down at the toilet, I noticed something on my body and immediately ran downstairs to show her. I said, "Babe, look at this."

I pointed to my right thigh where the pressure had been. There were five black and blue marks on my thigh that looked as if they have been made by five fingers!

"Oh my," was her response.

"Exactly," I said.

It wasn't until months later that the true meaning of this experience was revealed to me. I was driving to a job during the day and just daydreaming when this episode came into mind, and the revelation came that I wasn't punched, something was put into me by *it*. The Lord came and took back out what had been placed in my middle stomach area by evil to do me harm! I got so excited I called Sharmalie immediately and told her what had just been revealed to me. It is incredible what the Lord does and how He does it. When this stuff happens, it's unmistakable where it originated.

I'm so amazed at how many times the Lord has had an impact in my life. Some are direct results and recognizable to me like this event, although when I finally get to be with Him in heaven, He will reveal how many times He was involved and I didn't recognize it. It's only by His grace that I received these blessings both in the act of healing and recognition of the blessing so that I make no mistake that this was due to anything that I or man could have accomplished, only truly by the hand of God.

CHAPTER 10

Aaron Comes to the Lord

After our chat on Christmas Eve, Aaron and I had shorter chats, but he still hadn't decided to let the Lord in. However, something was about to happen to him that would change everything. Aaron now lived with his then girlfriend in an apartment. He was beginning to feel uncomfortable in the apartment and didn't know why. He was aware that I slept with a Bible on the bedside table, and I believe he knew these feelings were not of the natural kind. He did say that whatever was in the house lived in the master closet. At least that's where he felt he was always aware of it. His girlfriend told him that she would feel the need to cry and would always go in there to do it. She was not saved or even aware of the presence of the Lord as of yet. So Aaron took his newly received Bible and went into the closet to command the demon to leave. We had talked about doing this before, so he understood what to do.

I'm not sure, but I believe that *it* or maybe one that *it* controlled was sent to Aaron to ensure whatever he did he didn't find the truth of the Lord. This happened with Danielle, our daughter, so I expected *it* to eventually attack Aaron. He came over to visit one day to chat to his old man. We were sitting at the kitchen table when he began to tell me of a really weird dream he had. Neither of us at this time understood that this wasn't a dream but a vision that would be explained later to me by the Holy Spirit, and then I would interpret it to Aaron.

Aaron will explain this dream in detail during his story to follow. This event really ended up scaring him. I then followed up our conversation after a short pause, "Aaron, when you're ready, I'll show you how to come to the Lord for good."

I'll never forget that glorious moment when he looked at me and said, "I think I'm ready."

Immediately I said, "Mummy's upstairs. Let's go see her."

Sharmalie was dusting in an upstairs bedroom, and I just told her, "Babe, Aaron is ready to come to the Lord. Let's pray together."

Without any further words I said, "Let's kneel down and pray together."

I grabbed both of their hands and began to pray the prayer of salvation. I had Aaron repeat with his mouth the prayer. (When Aaron was getting ready to repeat the prayer, his breathing became very noticeable. It was like he had just finished running a short lap around the house.) I was so happy that I was squeezing their hands extremely hard, but I wanted the gravity of this situation to sink into them. At the end of the prayer I turned to Aaron and told him with a proud Daddy smile on my face, "Aaron, your name has been written into the Lamb's Book of Life. The angels have broken out into song about one more lost sheep coming home, and you will inherit eternal life with Him as He has promised!"

A Comment from Aaron in His Own Words

I was always an impressionable person. I looked up to people, loved their views, and listened to what they had to say. But the problem was when I had no knowledge on the subject at hand. These were the times I was able to mold to a particular point of view a bit easier.

My knowledge of religion was minimal. We never went to church growing up in my family. The only time I would enter a church at all was on Saturdays to deliver flowers for multiple churches on Sunday. I worked as a flower delivery guy at a local florist. When I entered these churches, I always felt out of place. No one was there on Saturdays. It was quiet with creaking wood. It just felt creepy.

For me, it starts just a couple years out of high school, twenty years old or so. One of my best friends at the time, Jennifer, was always a very smart person. I knew this about her, and it's probably why I was always so interested in things that she had to say and ideas she had to share. She had been taking a religion course in college that focused on multiple different views and beliefs of people from all over the world. With this new knowledge she would constantly share the way she felt about all of them. With no knowledge of them myself, I was all ears, respecting her opinions. Jenn was on a path for peace because that is what made sense in a world fighting and a country a few years into a war. Buddhism was her answer. She had visited a Buddhist temple for a few weeks to learn as much as she could. While she had amazing things to say about Buddhism, unfortunately other religions suffered her negative opinions, including Christianity. I don't blame her for how my views of Christianity were, but I blame myself for not seeking my own knowledge of it. Ideas in my head were of how it was ridiculous that a God created us and that evolution was a myth. All of these ideas were there because I had not experienced anything yet. At those times I wasn't ready to hear it, but those times were changing. Things would begin to start to make a bit too much sense for me to ignore. At this time Jenn and I had a falling out and didn't really talk anymore. It was a good three years before I would hear from her again.

Over the years I watched my father start to make the transition himself. He would sometimes talk to us about it, but I never felt like it was being pushed or anything. He started with a crucifix in his work van and the words "Jesus is Lord" on the back for everyone around him to see. He would tell me about how people would pull up to him at stoplights and just thank him for that message because they needed to hear it that day. It's funny how a message on the side of a van can be so powerful to the people who need it the most. It started with me just respecting things that my father asked of me like not using the Lord's name in vain. I was guilty of this transgression. It would slip out from time to time, but one day my father asked me not to. I knew right off the bat that it was something he was passionate about, so I respected that and never forgot it.

I had then started to see friends change in religious beliefs too, people I never really expected it from. One of my childhood friends, Shaun, had made this change very drastically. The change was so drastic to the point that other friends of ours would start to say things about him becoming a "Jesus freak." It bothered me on a new level when people would say things like this because I saw how invested he had become and how much it meant to him. I also thought it was disrespectful to this Jesus character that had been making such a big impact on the people close to me. Shaun would tell me about his experiences when he would pray. The way he described it sounded supernatural to me. This also started to grab my interest.

As more time passed for me, I made more of these life-changing observations in the people around me. One time I was heading to England with my parents to see all of my mother's side of the family. We were going to be celebrating Christmas and her fiftieth birthday out there with a pretty big party. It was combined with a few other friends' birthdays, so the attendance was expected to be in the few hundreds. Because of an ice storm that night, about a hundred people showed up. We had rented a hall with a stage, dance floor, food, drinks, and balloons, just a huge production. It was really great. All of the family was there, and no one was expecting what I had prepared for my mother on that day. I had written a song for her and played it for her at her party. This was a pretty big deal for me too, seeing how I had never performed in front of more than a handful of close friends before. Nor had my mother ever heard me sing to her. In these situations I would probably buckle under stage fright, but I had tried something that I never really had before. I prayed. In this time of nervousness and intimidation I felt confident and excited. I prayed before we left the house that this song that I had worked hard on would go amazing and perfect because that was what she deserved. I'm a big fan of surprises, and I not only surprised her and every single person there but also myself. That is the first time I think I took the power of prayer that I had heard so much about and applied it to my life. I feel I received a clear result that night. I would have been shaking nervous but was calm and ready instead.

Later in the week on Christmas Eve my mother went out to visit some of her old friends as my father and I went out for a snowy, icy walk to a local pub. It was one of the best times on record with my dad as far as quality time goes. The chat just started to begin with normal chitchat and guy talk. I can't recall how we got on the topic of the Lord, but I know once we were there, we ended up talking for quite a while. This is the time where I had started spitting out all of the questions that had been building up in my head. Sure, my dad didn't have all the answers right then and there, but I was completely content with every answer he gave. Each answer was filled with a certain peace that put my questions at ease, but I still wanted more. I saw my dad's face completely light up just because of the simple fact that I was even asking. My dad knew that I was on my way.

Shortly after I returned stateside, the weird stuff started happening. It took about a month's time before I decided I *knew* that what I was seeing and feeling was the real thing.

I had recently moved into an apartment with my girlfriend, Courtney, before the trip to England. Courtney had moved down from New York so that we could start moving our relationship to the next level. She stayed for only two weeks before she decided that she missed her friends and family and moved back. I was able to pay for this apartment myself, so I decided I was going to stay there since I was so close to my job.

At this point I had not talked to Jenn for years. One day out of the blue my phone rang. Her number popped up on my phone. She wasn't stored in my phone anymore, but I recognized the number. As I looked at who was calling me, I froze. I wasn't prepared for this. I didn't really know how to feel since I hadn't talked to her in a long time and was kind of bitter about it. I let it go to voice mail. All day I wondered why she might be calling me, but I had no idea. All I knew was that I wanted to give her an earful of my feelings and how messed up it was that we hadn't talked in so long. The next day I got a call again. This time I answered it with vigilance. I was curious to see why she was calling me.

She asked how I was doing, and she told me about herself. Jenn had come to the Lord in a powerful way, and once I began to realize that this was the reason for her calling, I immediately put my guard down. This made a lot of sense, certainly because of all the questions that I had started to have about the Christian faith. The part that struck me as odd first is that she just had a feeling out of nowhere that she needed to do this, call me, and tell me that she had come to the Lord and was able to answer questions to the best of her ability. She started by sending me a Bible with my initials on it. All I could think about was how impeccable her timing was. Waves of interest and questions hit me, and opportunities to have them answered were literally placed in my lap. I still had slight contact with Jenn for a couple months after that through a few e-mails with passages, advice, and questions, but I haven't heard from her for years. The contact she made was intentional by a higher power. This was becoming clear to me.

My apartment was a two-bedroom place. With 1,300 square feet, it pretty big for just me. As quiet as I liked my apartment, sometimes it just bugged me deep down. It felt like there was something else there and I wasn't alone. It felt like this so much to the point where it bothered me to sleep with my closet door open, and I had no idea why.

After Courtney went home to New York, we talked about our relationship and if we could make it work, but we grew weary of the long distance that we had kept between us for years. There was one thing that stuck out to me that she said and immediately turned another key in my head. While I was a work, Courtney mentioned how lonely she was because she wasn't working at the time. Sure, I can understand that. New home, new area, not many friends yet, I get it. She had mentioned to me that she would go into the closet in the master bedroom, sit on the floor, and cry. I had no knowledge of this happening while we were living together. Nor did I know why I felt weird about that closet, but when she told me this, it clicked again. There actually was something in that closet that felt dark, something that scared me, that had a heavy presence. Whatever it was, it was drawing her to the closet and overwhelming her.

As soon as this phone call with Courtney ended, I grabbed my Bible and used the words that my father had told me gave me power over these dark forces. I started in my closet, holding my Bible and repeating, "In the name of the Lord Jesus Christ, I command you to leave!"

I walked all over my apartment in every room, repeating this. When I had finished, I walked over to my couch with my Bible in my hand. I can't even describe the feeling that I felt at that moment. I felt the most tremendous weight lifted off of my entire body. The feeling was indescribable. I felt as light as a feather, and despite everything that was going on in my failed relationship, I knew that everything was completely fine.

Since that day I have slept with my Bible by my side. There was a certain level of comfort that it gave me. The feeling that something was looking out for me felt good. I felt like the Bible and those words I spoke were my gateway to that feeling.

Another one of my experiences happened in that apartment not more than a couple weeks after the last one. I had not yet been saved in the eyes of the Lord, so these dark entities were still hard at work. This time it was a dream that I had had. This wasn't an ordinary dream though. I generally have dreams that are clear, and I tend to remember them. But there was something about this dream that just felt more real than any other one I've ever had.

It started with my dad and me walking through a school hallway, not really saying much, but he was leading me through it. We walked out the back of the school, down a hill, and into the woods. The woods had an eerie feel to them. It was daytime but darker, overcast with bare-branched trees. We walked down to the bottom, which was flat. At the bottom we found a creek of stagnant, smelly water that look like it hadn't been touched in weeks. We moved along past it but then heard a frantic rustling behind us. As I turn around to look to see what all the commotion was, I saw a tent and a horribly ugly creature. The word *ugly* has taken on a new meaning to me since that dream. With the slightly contorted bodily shape of Gollum from *The Lord of the Rings* as well as the same color, this very angry creature was nothing short of hideously ugly. This creature was very violently grabbing the tent and shaking it. He did this with so much erratic force that even seeing it would frighten you. As my dad and I watched this happen in shock, the only words that came out of my mouth were, "What the—" Before I could get out any more than that, the creature stopped with the tent and snapped its head around to look at me. As quickly as I noticed it there, it had grabbed me by the back of my shirt, and then it was trying to drag me into the stagnant, smelly water next to us. Being just as aggressive, he was yanking and tugging at my shirt while I struggled to get away. Just before I felt any of that water touch me, I shot up from my bed and gasped for air. I woke up from the dream and noticed the physical feeling of my shirt being pulled from the back. I am absolutely convinced that I caught my shirt being pulled as I was waking up. I felt it in my consciousness. I immediately grabbed my Bible and used those powerful words again, "In the name of the Lord Jesus Christ, I command you to leave!"

I said it with more power and passion than I ever had before. The first time I used those words, I felt the weight lifted, but this time was different. I felt the power they had behind them. It gave me confidence, even though I was completely terrified seconds prior.

At this point I had had enough. I would ask myself, "How much more proof do you need?" The next morning I traveled to my parents' house to tell them about all the things that had been happening to me and the feelings I had been having. My dad's face just started to light up when I began to tell him because he knew that today was the day that I was coming to the Lord. That was the day that I recited the prayer of salvation and accepted Jesus Christ as my Lord and Savior.

Each time one of these occurrences would happen, it all just made too much sense for me to ignore. I was looking for the proof, and I began to realize that it was being given to me because I was asking for it. If I ever feel like I have an absence of God in my life, I ask for guidance. Without fail, it shows up. An opportunity or development is shown to me that is without doubt just too obvious to ignore. Instances like this do tend to happen in my life still, but they are often geared toward things that prevent me from bringing someone else closer to the Lord. As for me, I feel protected and understand these things for exactly what they are. For me it's more and more proof, but for other people it is meant to slow them down. It is almost as if I understand life on a different level. People will come to the Lord when they are ready, and they shouldn't feel pushed. I wouldn't be as passionate about it if it wasn't completely my decision. Even if I don't know the Bible inside and out, my job is to tell my story and share my experiences in the hopes that other people will soon feel the inner peace that is God's love. God loves all of us, and if everyone felt that, this world would be a much different place.

What a blessing from the Lord bringing the final member or our little family to Him. When Aaron forwarded his thoughts to me so that I could include them in our story, I read his review of the dream he had had. This was the first time I had seen written down the full dream revealed. I'm positive these thoughts were given to me by the Holy Spirit, and I'm giving Him the credit because of the rapid-fire understanding of the dream that I had, much faster than I could have realized the truth in my little bits of knowledge.

By the Holy Spirit, this is what was given to me. The school hallway is a place of learning. In his dream I was leading Aaron through this hallway because I was to teach him the way to the Lord. We went down the hill away from the Lord and the truth of the Bible to show him where he was currently headed. The bare trees represent the lack of fruit in life without the Lord. A smelly stream represents sin. It is foul in odor, untouched by the goodness of the Lord. The creature is a demon that knew Aaron and was responsible for preventing him from finding the truth of the Bible. Just as it was when Moses brought Israel out of Egypt, the tent was used as the holy temple of God, storing the Ark of the Covenant. In a sense this is true today of Christians and our faith in the Lord. In other words, the creature was violently shaking Aaron's tent of faith, his protection from evil, and this creature did not want the tent to stand. When Aaron spoke, he uncovered his fallen nature again, and the creature could now see him but not me, as I was covered by the blood of Christ. By grabbing Aaron by the shirt and pulling him, it was trying to drag him into the smelly water representing sin; however, he awoke before any of the water could touch him. The Lord knew that the following day he would be eternally delivered from sin by confessing Jesus as his Lord and Savior.

When I am shown visions or given information by the Lord through the Holy Spirit, I pray that I'm given the discernment to recognize when I am communicated with from the Lord. I say, "Lord, You know me and the fact that I'm as thick as two short planks of wood. Please make it so clear that when You're showing me something, I recognize it as being from You."

He knows this and surely does make it known that these are from Him and not from my own thoughts. Did you know that the Holy Spirit speaks to you through your thoughts? These are just that—thoughts, not physically hearing. The question really is this: How can you recognize that it's Him and not you? This discernment comes through prayer, asking for the Lord to make it clear to you. In this case of Aaron's vision, I was sitting at our kitchen table and reading Aaron's vision for the second time because I was not sure what it meant or even that it was a vision after the first reading. Then my eyes wandered off of the pages, and I found myself looking toward the floor but not really seeing anything around me. My thoughts went to the beginning of the dream when I was leading him through a school hallway, and like a lightning bolt, a thought came out very strongly. *It's a place of learning.* (This phrase is not found anywhere in the vision.) It was if someone had actually said this to me without me actually physically hearing any comment. I jolted back to reality and spoke it out load, saying just that. I began to read his vision again, and everything else was made clear as I read it line by line. Quickly I jotted down notes as I read it so that I would not forget the understanding.

There have been other instances where this has taken place, and I have been shown enough times that when the Holy Spirit is conveying a message to me, I know where it's coming from. For example, the name of the book was changed by the Lord Himself through the Holy Spirit delivering the message to me. One morning in the early stages of writing the book, I awoke, wiped the sleep from my eyes, and said out loud, "Okay, Lord, I'll do that."

I had been given a command to change the name of the book to *Saving My Family*. The first title was something really strange and weak in composition. The Lord changed that, and I obeyed. I got up and went downstairs to the computer and changed the name of the book right then.

I would also like to add here that I chose throughout our story not to chase out demons by standing in front of my family members and casting out the demons in Jesus' name. Yes, this certainly does work; however, as far as I understand it, when demons are cast out this way, if a person does not come to the Lord at that time, confessing with his or her mouth to Jesus as Lord and Savior, the demon can come back with help, perhaps with seven other demons. I chose to offer praises and worship as my tool against these dark forces. The Lord did not let me down. In the beginning our God spoke everything into existence. This is why one must say the sinner's prayer or prayer of salvation by using his or her mouth to confess to God, for what the mouth says is in the heart.

CHAPTER 11

Blessing with Holy Oil

The Bible mentions anointing oil many times throughout the Bible. "And they cast out demons and anointed with oil many who were sick and healed them" (Mark 6:13). "Then you shall take the anointing oil and anoint the tabernacle and all that is in it, and you shall hallow it and all its utensils, and it shall be holy" (Exodus 40:9). Psalm 23:1–6 also says,

> A psalm of David, the Lord is my Shepherd; I shall not want. He makes me lie down in green pastures. He leads me beside still waters. He restores my soul. He leads me in paths of righteousness for His name's sake. Yea, though I walk through the valley of the shadow of death, I will fear no evil, for You are with me, your rod and your staff, they comfort me. You prepare a table before me in the presence of my enemies; You anoint my head with oil; my cup runs over.

It was now time to begin to implement our plan to get right with the Lord. Sharmalie now again departed to England, and I was alone at home. I was really tired of going through this stuff, and I was now actively following the plan to clean up our lives spiritually.

I went golfing with Darrell for the day and asked him if he could bring some holy oil with him so that I might use some to bless the house. He knew about the problems I was having. We usually talked about once a week, generally on Monday morning. Well, like a good minister he brought the holy oil; however, when we were finishing up, it was turning dark. I knew *it* was waiting at home for me. I didn't want to go through another night like all of the others. Thankfully Darrell agreed to come back to the house with me so that we could complete the blessing together. I told him, "Don't be surprised if weird stuff happens while we're doing this."

We arrived at the house well past sunset, and as we were standing in the driveway, he handed me the oil. I raised it to God and asked Him to bless this oil. I just wanted to be sure this was the real deal. We began by blessing the garage doors on the outside and then moved to the front door on the outside. I suspect that actually this is all the Lord needed, but I wasn't sure. We went in, and I continued to bless the house above every door and window, even closets, while Darrell walked with me, praying to the Lord, saying, "Father God, give dominion of this house to this man. Let no evil return here."

Trust me when I tell you it worked! I slept without the lights on. I no longer felt a presence in the house. The radio has not changed stations since. Evil had been cast out and could no longer linger or move about freely. That's a critical statement. Evil can still enter when you invite in someone who is not saved, but it's not free to move around or stay. Actually that person may feel a bit uneasy in the house and not understand why. This would be true of any blessed home.

Some time passed, and Aaron purchased a home of his own. I now understand those bumper stickers that say, "They are not really moved out until they get all of their junk out of the basement." How true, how true! Now that Aaron had his new home and with everything we had all lived through, I asked him if he wanted me to bless his house. He quickly agreed. Sharmalie and I arrived at the house, dropped off some more stuff into the garage, and quickly gathered Aaron to accomplish the most important item on the list. With the three of us together, I said, "Let's go downstairs to the front door and start there."

In this condo there was a stairwell to the main door. It was unshared by any other home, and it only opened to Aaron's new home. As we got to the bottom of the stairs at the front door, we noticed that the entry light inside of the hall was not working.

"Must be burned out," I said. "No matter. We'll just continue. You can change that later."

The three of us bowed our heads in prayer, and I asked the Lord to bless this house with us. I took the holy oil, put some on my index finger, raised it up to the upper door trim, and said, "I bless this house in the name of the Father, the Son, and the Holy Spirit."

While I was saying this, I made the sign of the cross with the holy oil on the trim above the door. The exact moment I finish with the prayer and the sign of the cross, the burned-out light came on! We just quickly looked at each other and began laughing. Talk about the Lord's perfect timing. He's always available at the right time.

If you're wondering where you can get the holy oil, there are many ways. Ask your local pastor or priest first. When I was desperate to bless the house, I ran all over the place, rushing from church to church to see if I could find someone who would give me a sampling of the oil. Nobody was ever around. We were not members of the church yet. I had seen vials in Christian bookstores as well. Just make sure either you bless the oil before you use it, or have your pastor do it before you trust its effectiveness. Ours smell of frankincense and myrrh. It's an absolutely beautiful scent, truly heaven-sent.

The blessing of your home, cars, and/or possessions, I believe, is a critical element to fight evil. To me, it was an important step in having a safe place away from evil that I *know* they cannot ignore. Becoming stronger in the Lord by faith and developing a passion to grow in Him and work for Him by spreading His Word to whomever will listen, you become a threat to evil, and these creatures will now begin to take notice. Have you ever had anything happen like the situations that I experienced? I'll bet so if you are saved by the blood of Christ. You may just not know, understand, or recognize the situation for what it really is. I'm trying to convey the importance of this tool from God. Remember back when I was with my mother in the last moments of life and I told of how she sat up and turned toward the priest when he was about to give her last rites with the holy oil on his finger? God gave this tool for believers to use in His name.

This may sound strange or out of this world, but *it* still comes back to the house. *it* cannot enter and must certainly be disappointed. How do I know this? I would be able to walk into a room and feel *its* presence. Well, this time was not on the inside. However, I felt *it* come to the outside of the house where I was located while I was on the inside. During the three times I felt *it*, my response was nothing but prayer. I would ask the Father to send an angel and chase *it* away. The feeling of relief afterward is always remarkable. It's not just a simple feeling. These are heavy, dreadful, fearful feelings. Something is definitely not right, and I can look toward a specific place. It's the kind of feeling you have when the hair on the back of your neck stands up, but nobody is really around or close to you. Although, I've not had this experience in any place other than my own home. The Lord has sharpened my iron, my sword in the armor of God. I feel as though He has created a warrior attitude in me. "What is your sword?" One might ask. It's the Word of the Bible, and this is the sword in the armor of God. I used to be quite fearful during these episodes. Now I am just plain aggressive at chasing it away, for I know who is in me.

I'd like to take a moment to review what the armor of God is, as it's found in the New King James version of the Bible. Ephesians 6:11–20 says,

> Put on the whole armor of God, that you may be able to stand against the wiles of the devil. For we do not wrestle against flesh and blood, but against principalities, against powers, against the rulers of the darkness of this age, against spiritual hosts of wickedness in heavenly places. Therefore take up the whole armor

of God, that you may be able to withstand in the evil day, and having done all, to stand. Stand therefore, having girded your waist with truth, having put on the breastplate of righteousness, And having shod your feet with preparation of the gospel of peace; Above all, taking the shield of faith which you will be able to quench all the fiery darts of the wicked one. And take the helmet of salvation, and the sword of the Spirit, which is the word of God; Praying always with prayer and supplication in the Spirit, being watchful to this end with all perseverance and supplication for all the saints And for me, that utterance may be given to me, that I may open my mouth boldly to make known the mystery of the gospel. For which I am ambassador in chains; that in it I may speak boldly, as I ought to speak.

CHAPTER 12

Everything Is Part of God's Plan

L et's get back to our plan. The whole family was now saved. Ours, Danielle, and now Aaron's houses had all been blessed as well as cars and the plane. The next item was our marriage, which had to be completed in the eyes of the church. We had not yet started going to our local church, so my friend Darrell was our best option. With the date set, our second—truly our first—marriage was now about fifteen days away. However, *its* little plan began to take shape. Remember when I was punched in the gut while I was lying in bed? Before the Lord came to take back out what evil had put in, however, what was put inside me began to take shape in the form of an ambulance ride to the hospital (my first in fifty-seven years of life) for an appendix that had decided it didn't want to be part of me anymore. I believe there was more harm done to me, but the Lord interceded on my behalf, removing other aliments before they had the chance to metastasize. He left the appendix issue to work for His good.

This happened March of 2012. Fifteen days before we were to complete another item on the list to get right under God, the evil creature brings this incident in an attempt to stop us from reaching our goal. God works in many ways, even using evil's means to achieve His goals. This is what was about to happen. Everything was set for the wedding. Danielle was ready to come up with our grandson. Darrell was all set on the date, and plans had been made. And then this happened. The hospital stay was short, only two days, but the appendix ruptured when they tried to remove it and it took them longer to clean me up. It was horrible. They used gas to blow me up like a balloon so that it was easier for them to move around in there, but the procedure made me so uncomfortable even after I got home, I was sure Sharmalie thought, *Oh, great. They're putting more gas in him. He doesn't need that.* I had to sleep on the couch with my legs up. It was the only place I felt comfortable in the house. The bigger concern was that I could not eat anything. For seven days all I had was one bite of a banana and some yogurt, maybe a spoonful or so. Sharmalie also commented, "I'll be so happy when you ask me to make you spaghetti again." I can't get enough of the stuff!

How was the Lord going to use this for His purposes? Sharmalie even asked a few times, "Shall we postpone the wedding?"

"Absolutely not!" was always my answer, I *knew* where this was coming from and was determined not to let *it* win. Why did this happen? Here's one reason. Before the appendix episode, I had gained enough weight that my wedding ring would not fit on the day we were to be married. Neither did Sharmalie's, but because I was not eating as much during this recovery time, I lost twelve pounds in a week. Not only did mine fit on my hand, but because of the stress involved, so did Sharmalie's! Had this not happened, those rings would not have fit onto our fingers, and *it* might have won. *It* didn't though. The Lord works in wondrous ways, doesn't He?

Darrell performed the ceremony here at the house with me in stretchy sports pants. That's all I could stand around my waist. Danielle even brought the veil from her wedding so that her mummy could wear it. You see, we never had one, so Sharmalie had no memories of a wedding dress to fall back on. Great thinking, Danielle! Aaron even played the wedding march through his iPhone. It brought me to tears. Again we didn't have that. Aaron walked Sharmalie in from the kitchen with Danielle and our grandson, Owen, as ring bearer! What beautiful gifts from God weddings are. I told Sharmalie the evening she came to Christ that *our love would become stronger than she could possibly imagine*, and it has, growing more and more since that day. We often look deeply at each other at night, and I sometimes say, "Babe, we'll know each other and the kids for an eternity." What a wonderful thought.

Steve and Sharmalie, with Darrell administering
the vows and Cynthia looking on

Aaron, Owen, and Danielle watching us getting married

The happy couple

Our wedding—Darrell, Steve, Sharmalie, and Cynthia

CHAPTER 13

The Lord Gives Sharmalie a Sign

Aaron had begun to be put into his trial. The Lord started to take his little world apart at the seams. He was in a business partnership with another that began to fall apart. His girlfriend at the time decided to call it quits, which absolutely devastated Aaron. He closed himself off from the world, and we had a hard time getting in touch with him, which in today's age should not be difficult. When we did talk to him, Sharmalie was the one to get through. He was crying over the phone. That made her cry. When they hung up with each other, we were really worried and concerned for our son. It's one of those times you just don't know what to do with yourself. No matter where you move in the house, it seems to be just as bad. You can't concentrate. Sharmalie couldn't take it. She said she was going outside, just trying to run, but in this case her action was by divine design. It was an absolutely beautiful, windless, calm evening with thousands of stars out. She went out into the street and looked up to the stars and began to cry and pray. Remember, this is a windless evening. Suddenly she was surrounded by a swirling wind that made her nightie swirl up and around her! She came in from outside slightly breathless and told me what just had happened. We had some previous conversations when she would say, "Why does all this stuff happen to you and never me?"

She can no longer say that. The Lord used His finger to swirl that wind around her to let her know, "*Be still and know that I am*!"

It was also during this time that the Holy Spirit woke me from a deep sleep in the middle of the night with a strong feeling to pray for Aaron right now. That was an easy command to complete. The Daddy side of me was greatly concerned, but the spiritual side knew that everything would be just fine.

To add to this trying time, Aaron called me a few days later, crying. He said something, and at first all I heard is "killed himself." I thought the worst and sat up. I asked, "What are you saying?"

It turned out that a close friend of his, someone he had grown up with, had just committed suicide with a pistol and the father had found him in his apartment surrounded by pictures of his young daughters. What a shame that no one knew. Could we have made a difference in what he was feeling? We can only pray for the children that he left behind.

CHAPTER 14

Keep Your Eyes on Jesus

A few months later I went to bed first one evening. This happened a lot! Lying there in the bed, facing a wall in our bedroom with my eyes closed, just beginning to rest but still fully awake, suddenly I saw a different wall not our bedroom wall in front of me, but I'm looking at it as if from the same prone position on my side. With my eyes still closed, the wall I'm seeing is in the daylight, but its night time now that I'm going to bed. It had an off-white color to it. Because I'm a painter, I recognized it as shell white, and there were red roses with long stems placed evenly throughout the wall spaced about eighteen inches apart. I also saw the shadow of a palm tree gently blowing in the breeze on this wall. Again I was seeing this as if I was actually looking at it truly in front of me. I had a hard time understanding and believing what I was seeing. After all, I was still awake with my eyes closed. I forced my eyes closed to make sure they were actually closed. Yep, they were, and I looked back at the wall, it was all still there. Then I opened my eyes to just check and see our bedroom wall, ya there's our wall, so I hurried to close my eyes again, but the vision was gone.

What a mistake to open my eyes. I'm sure that if I had chosen to look around, I would have seen more, but the lack of faith in what the Lord wanted to show me stopped the vision. That's true with our faith. If you stop believing, He stops showing. Believe that our Lord has you, and don't give up keeping your eyes on Him through faith. I tried in my own way to figure out the meaning of this vision, saying stupid stuff like, "What horrible wallpaper," or, "Hey, babe, the Lord is showing me we are going on vacation to someplace with palm trees."

That couldn't be further from the truth. I've heard Dr. David Jerimiah teach that every event casts a shadow, teaching about the coming return of our Lord. So in this vision He was sending a message to me, but what was it?

I received that answer a short time after the event in the form of reading a book titled *My Time in Heaven*, which was written by Richard Sigmund. He tells his story of actually dying in a car accident, being taken to heaven, and being shown things to write about so that others would know them. Well, while I was reading a chapter titled "Memorials, the Way of the Rose," I saw that one sentence referred to some of the homes he was shown in heaven. It says, "They had many spacious rooms, decorated with rose-colored woodwork." I sat up. Could it be that the Lord was showing me a home in heaven that we would occupy someday? Mr. Sigmund talked many times about roses in heaven. There was even a street named Rose Way. Well, I was pretty sure the Lord was trying to tell me or show me something about heaven and how it connected to my life. Even if it was just the fact that I would see this someday. In my prayers with the Lord I let Him know that when He takes me to my mansion, I am going to run in to find that wall! Oh, by the way after I read Mr. Sigmund's book, I no longer thought that rose wallpaper looked ugly!

In my previous analogy of using an old-time phone and being steadfast in waiting for an answer from God, this is where I hung up early. Even after all of the signs and wonders He has allowed me to have in my life, again I failed. I opened my eyes. This is a simple case of not being properly prepared for the information our Lord was willing to share with me. I am learning though. I am defeating the evil that has been challenging my life only through the Word of the Bible and strong faith in Him.

This situation is akin to the story of Jesus approaching the boat on the seas in the midst of a storm and walking on water. He called to Peter to come to Him on the open waters. Peter obeyed and was able to walk on water as long as he kept his eyes upon Jesus. When he looked down, removing his eyes from Jesus and looking at the water below, his faith faltered, and rather than seeing Jesus, he saw his situation and sank into the sea. The way I handled this vision happened in the exact way Peter failed at walking on water. I took my eyes off Him. By removing my eyes and weakening my faith, I sank back into reality, seeing my situation in my earthly bedroom instead of seeing one that I might someday occupy in heaven. Throughout our story most of the visits or visions I received from our Lord were at times when I was *ready to listen*. In other words, *I was quiet, at rest, and ready to listen*. It's difficult for us to maintain our eyes on Jesus when times are hard, but that's what's required. Rely on Him in all things and keep Him in sight.

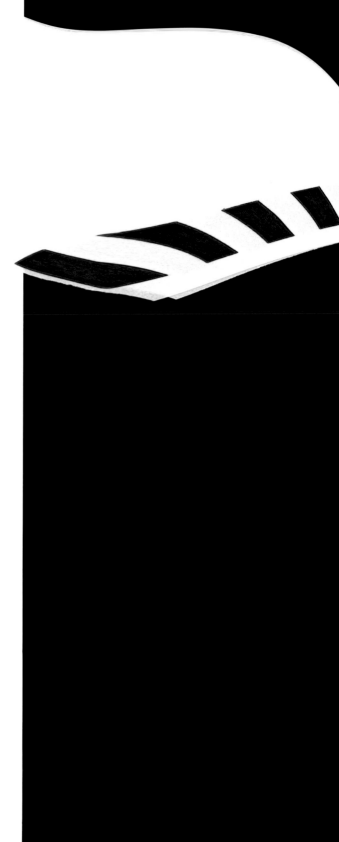

CHAPTER 15

Being under Authority

A s we followed our plan, the next amazing thing happened, and I'm sure the Holy Spirit was working in Sharmalie. She was truly under His guidance. Early in 2012 she said to me, "We need to be going to church!" She just proclaimed our path and final step of the original plan to get straight with God. She already knew where we were supposed to go, and I gladly agreed. As a matter of fact, after she finished saying this, she walked around the corner, and I literally jumped for joy, looking toward heaven and blessing His name and work in our lives. What I had thought would never happen a short time ago had now come to pass. We were going to church as a couple under God! Actually the seed had been planted by two good friends of ours, Rob and Karen Bentall. Karen had been inviting Sharmalie to go to this church for movie nights, not sermons, just watching and discussing movies. This introduced Sharmalie to some people in what would become our church. Church is the people inside the walls, not the building itself, so Sharmalie was already being prepared for what she had just proclaimed. One never really knows how actions or simple

words can affect somebody and hopefully bring another person to the Lord.

To be under authority is critical in your walk with God. The line of authority is God, Jesus, church, man, and woman. There's no need to be politically correct here. This is the way God designed it—each under authority of the one before and responsible to God. When Eve ate the apple and handed it to Adam, the Devil knew that this was the way to go against God's authority, breaking the chain. When they sinned and God walked down into the garden, looking for them, He called out, "Adam, where are you?" He did not call out for Eve. It was Adam who had allowed his family to come under sin by not following God's commandments. He was responsible for Eve and the actions of the family. Up until our total conversion to the Lord as a family, I followed in those sinful footsteps. I was not teaching, pastoring, and growing my family in the commandments under the authority of the church. That is now set right.

We love our local pastors, Knox and Bev Swayze. They are good people who have had their own struggles and who know the Word of the Lord, and I believe they teach it in the correct way. I would like to add here that we, man and woman, are equally created under God, each with different responsibilities under God. Yes, women are to submit to the men, but that does not mean they must submit blindly without a say in the family's decisions, although the men are ultimately responsible to God for those decisions. Think of Adam eating the apple from Eve. The Bible states, "Wives, submit to your own husbands, as to The Lord. For the husband is the head of the wife, as also Christ is head of the church; and He is the Savoir of the body. Therefore, just as the church is subject to Christ, so let the wives be to their own husbands in everything" (Ephesians 5:22–24). Submitting to the man, I believe, also does not entail following him blindly if he is leading the family into sin. She then may not submit to the man who invites sin into the family's life. There are many women who are used throughout the Bible in extremely important times. Today women are used as they were then by our Lord. In our case, Bev is one of our teachers of the Word of the Lord, teaching to the multitudes through one of His faithful servants. Knox and Bev are our copastors, and we willingly submit to their authority as leaders of our church family.

You must be careful in today's world that you're getting the true Word and meaning of the Bible. Jesus said that in the end times (which we are in) "many would come in my name, to lead my sheep astray." Here's a word of caution. In your walk with the Lord, make sure you stay true to the Bible, and you do not stray from the truth. You can only know this by knowing the Word of the Bible, and then the Holy Spirit will work to teach you what's right and wrong. Know the Bible! Our favorite teachers include Dr. David Jerimiah, Joseph Prince, Dr. Charles Stanley, Ravi Zacharias, and our local pastors, Knox and Bev Swayze, copastors of Covenant Presbyterian Church of Manassas, Virginia. The full list appears in the front of the book. I would like to guide as many as possible to these teachers whom I believe teach the truth of the Word of the Bible.

Sharmalie and I are always ready to go to church to hear the Word of our Lord and to fellowship with like-minded believers. This is critical in your growth in God. The support that your local church gives is measured in how you grow in Him. If you're not growing and not motivated, you might want to look elsewhere. For me I need to have a teacher and not a preacher. By that I'm saying that I like to have a teacher take a verse of Scripture, break it down, and explain its meaning to me. Some are preachers who spend most of the time talking and not teaching the meaning of what's written in the Bible. To be under the authority of the church is keeping the chain in the right line. The Lord can then use you more in His purposes for His glory. Aaron wanted to give money to a charity a while back, and I told him, "That's a worthy thing, but let me ask you this: Who gets the glory? You or God?"

He thought before he answered, but I didn't let him get that far. I let him know that by being under the authority of the church, if he gave a tithe or an offering and the church then gave that to the needy, God would get the glory.

He said, "Yeah, but I feel guilty if I can't give enough at church."

I said, "That doesn't matter."

I related the story Jesus told of the old woman who put into the collection plate the smallest amount of money of that day, but it was all that she had. Others who were well off gave more, but they only offered a small amount of what they had. Jesus told His disciples, "Truly, truly I tell you, this old woman gave more than the rest. She gave all that she had. The others gave out of their abundance." The point sunk in. Aaron would soon begin to go to church, but it would not be steadily yet. The Holy Spirit would have to work on his heart on this point. Danielle, too, had to move her family into this arena.

Sharmalie and I were invited to our church youth group to tell our story. The kids ranged in age from twelve to eighteen. That's the scariest thing you can do—talk to a bunch of young folks who have no inhibitions about asking tough questions about your experiences. It turned out well, I believe. They really listened and asked thoughtful questions. A young lady asked one question I'll never forget. She asked, "How do you know God hears you?"

In turn I asked her, "Who do you pray to?"

She said, "God."

I then asked her, "And where is He?"

She thought about it for a second, and with a quick eye glance upward after a very short pause she said, "In me."

I just looked at her and smiled. She had her answer.

As a part of being under authority and being the man and the head of the family, in an effort to keep Jesus first in our lives, I placed Jesus first at the one of the most important times of the year to remember Him. I have a practice that I have started with my family that I would like to share. It has a special place in my heart too. Every Christmas the very first thing I do is share with my family something I have named the "First Gift of Christmas." It is simply a short sermon I deliver for inspiration through the Word of the Bible. If possible, we do this as a family before we go to church on Christmas Eve. On that day and time everything seems so special. We are together, sharing love during the Lord's birthday. The best music possible is on every radio station, so before we share in the fun of opening gifts, which He has enabled us to provide to all of our loved ones, we share thoughts about Him, as we should. We put Jesus first. I use this as an opportunity to teach and to cement the correct meaning of the Bible as I have learned it and to impart who I am anew to my wife and children and their families. Unlike our pastors, it takes me months to develop this chat. I want it right because I want to move them along the path and I want it to be relevant to the world or life events at that time. It's custom-fitted. (An example of my 2012 first gift of Christmas is in the appendix found at the end of the book.)

Now that we are going to church, I have had to step up to the plate; however, I do this gleefully by tithing to support the church's financial needs and by giving back to the Lord what He has given me either in talents or materials. Keeping my ears open to the Lord's words, we began planting the mustard seeds for financial blessings from the Lord. By tithing the Lord will bless you more financially than He will if you don't. How do you expect to receive a financial harvest from the Lord if you're not planting the financial seeds in church?

For me talents include my business skills as a painter, window cleaner, and such. I offer these services for the church with no expectation of payment. It's at my cost and labor. I look for opportunities to do this. We're not loaded with buckets full of money. Sometimes we only have about a hundred bucks in the bank; however, we still tithe.

Some time ago I got tired of having dreams of being a pilot and never acting on it. Now I was ready to use that passion for God. I joined the Civil Air Patrol and began doing search and rescue operations, using small general aviation aircraft like Cessna 182s. It wasn't long after I had started before the pilot flying us around on a training mission and honing our skills looked at me and said, "Would you like to fly the plane?" I enthusiastically agreed! I took the controls with his guidance, and I was hooked. Long story short I went on to get my pilots license, bought our first plane after only my second lesson, and then sold that one, and we now own our second plane. These were not expensive. I bought our first plane for $16,000 and the second one for $34,000, which is about the same cost as a car these days. It's a great injustice when individuals say that people who own planes are rich. I'm living proof that's not true. Why do I tell you this? During this phase of our story I prayed that the Lord would allow me to use this aircraft for His glory. I looked for ways to do this. I joined an organization called Pilots for Christ (pilotsforchrist.org), an international organization that looks for opportunities to give free flights to those with medical needs and to evangelize using the aircraft. What a fun way to serve our Lord. What a great opportunity to serve Him by doing something both Sharmalie and I love to do.

I still felt I was shortchanging the Lord with this gift and prayed for more. Shortly after that prayer our local pastor Knox called and asked if I would fly him to see an inmate at a prison in southern Virginia, a man whom he knew was having some troubles. Boy did I jump on that one. I said, "Let's work on the dates." I had to pick out some time when I would have enough money for the gas to cover it. I really did not have to worry about that. The Lord provided enough work so that we could make the trip. It saved Knox about three and a half hours' worth of driving time with just an hour and fifteen-minute flight each way.

They're like little time machines, and they save you all kinds of time. Little did I know what the Lord had in mind for me during this trip. I thought I was just the pilot driver to get Knox there so that he could do the Lord's work. He had something in mind for me too. The prison chaplain picked us up at the airport when we landed and drove us up to the prison. Things were about to get serious. We could see the double-razor wire walls with the curled barbed wire on top as well as guard towers and stone buildings on the inside grounds. You can take nothing inside of the prison with you—no ID, no wallet, no phone, nothing, just your clothes thankfully—but even with that, you're still scanned. After the security check area you walk through one inner door, and there you are facing the main fence gate into the inner yard. One opens, and you walk in between the gates. The first one closes with a clink. What a horrible sound it must be to those who are going to stay here for real, hearing that metal click and knowing there's no going back out until your time is done. Now the second gate opened, and we could walk into the inner yard. Just as we go about thirty feet inside the final gate, we saw a red line painted on the sidewalk running parallel to the fences about the width of a yellow line on the street. The chaplain informed us if anything happened that shouldn't be happening, we needed to get on the fence side of the red line. Everybody else wearing an orange jump suit who got on the fence side of the line would get shot!

Okay, this was for real now. Well, Knox went into a room with the inmate we came to see and tried to help him back onto the road and let him know that somebody cared. Our pastors do an awful lot of work that we really never see. Give them a word of encouragement. They need it as much as anybody else, maybe even more. In the meantime I walked with the chaplain, and he asked if I would like to see inside the dorms.

"Sure," I said.

We went inside of a dorm that was typically saved for veterans who had gotten themselves into hot water. There were about sixty beds in here and a central guard building with a clear view inside the area. We walked around as he showed me the area, and many approached us and wanted to talk. They knew who the chaplain was, so our conversation leaned toward the Lord, which was great!

We stopped to listen to a class they were having at the front of the building, and because I was unsure of the rules, I stopped where one inmate was sitting near his bunk. An incredibly loud horn tooted twice, and the inmate immediately jumped up and said to me, "Sir, sorry that's me, sir."

And then moved away. They are not allowed to be behind us within arm's reach. Wow, I knew I was somewhere I had never been before.

We offered what comfort we could and moved on. He told me, "We are going to see an inmate in the infirmary who has been diagnosed with terminal cancer. They are trying to get him an early release."

In this place everything was still a jail cell, even though you may be sick. He was in bad shape. He had lost all kinds of weight, but when we talked with him, we found out that he knew the Lord. We had a stimulating chat about getting to see Him soon. He wanted to get out but didn't want to go home. He just did not have any support there. That will wake you up to some hardships that you don't think about until you're confronted with them. While I was talking to him, I told him how I prayed and asked him about what he prayed for. It turned out that he didn't pray for himself. He said, "I pray that my daughter finds the Lord."

I looked deeply into his eyes and told him how I sometimes ended my prayers when I have something I'd like the Father to hear.

"Holy Spirit, carry this prayer to the Father's ears so that He may hear."

I let him know that God would hear him today. His eyes filled up with water. The three of us prayed together while the chaplain grabbed his hands and laid his head on the inmate's chest. What a powerful moment. That was my purpose here. It was not only to be a pilot driver for Knox. The Lord uses you as He sees fit. I'm so glad to be a part of His plan. Here are some pictures from that day—our plane, outside of the prison, and Knox and Steve flying back.

Our plane

Outside of the prison

Knox and Steve flying back

CHAPTER 16

The Bow and Arrow

A few months later, again while I was lying in the bed asleep, I was made aware of looking at myself from the outside, yet I was on the inside of my body at the same time. It was really weird, but that's how it was. I saw me standing there with my left arm fully extended out in front of me and my right arm cocked back with my hand near my right ear, looking forward at where my left hand was aimed. I then said, "Satan, I rebuke you!" in a firm, loud, commanding voice without fear. I don't normally remember dreams, so remembering them makes these occurrences stick out. Again the purpose of these visions is never clear at the moment they happen. I believe they are foreshadows of things to come.

Some time passed, and I started listening to a sermon by Dr. Charles Stanley on putting on the whole armor of God. At the same time I happened to be reading, looking at pictures really of places and stories from the Old and New Testament. It's a book of a great collection of the paintings from the true masters of painting, and I happened onto a drawing from Egypt of an archer in the shooting position ready to fire off his arrow. It was like a lightning bolt hit, and the revelation inside me became clear. It's truly impressive how the Lord does this. He knew I'd be listening and reading this book at the same time, and He knew I would make a correlation to the vision. I saw me shooting an arrow, but an arrow of what? How do you rebuke the Devil with an arrow? When I talked to Sharmalie, I told her I believed that something bad was headed our way and the Lord was warning me to be ready; however, listening to Dr. Stanley talking about the armor of God, I realized that the items in the armor of God were mostly defensive weapons, with the exception of the sword (which is the written Word of the Bible), and the sword can be used in an offensive and defensive manner to strike or to protect. Arrows aren't mentioned in the armor of God, so what was it? I wondered about this for a while, but after I wrote this book, I realized and *believe the Lord was showing me this: In our story the sword is the Word of God. This book is the bow, the means to deliver the arrow. The recounting of what our events tell others is the arrow that rebukes Satan! Just as the Bible does so well, so does any writing that stays true to the Word and puts Satan in his place under the authority of God. The reason I didn't see any bow or arrow in my vision is because this book was not yet written. It is now, so if I saw that vision again, the bow and the arrow would be in place.* Many times before I began to write the book, I struggled with and prayed about how to tell our story. I even wondered if I should tell it at all. The Lord settled that one day when I knew that this was to be done. I had a passion to begin to put into words our story. It was hard for Sharmalie to break me away from the computer once I began. My goal is get this book into as many willing hands as possible to serve the Lord's purposes. Realizing this purpose is so exciting. It's hard to sit here and type without a smile on my face. As a matter of fact, I am going to smile, knowing what I'm doing glorifies the Lord and rebukes Satan. I pray that the Lord might use me in this way to accomplish His work here in the end times.

In my morning read of the Bible just flipping through the pages, looking for what to read and review for the morning. I was going through the book of Psalms, and as I passed Psalm 64, it stuck out like a sore thumb. Something told me that this psalm was important. I had never read this psalm before this time, and I was shocked at how it correlated to our story. Psalm 64 as written in the King James Version is as follows:

> Oppressed by the wicked but rejoicing in The Lord.
> Hear my voice. O God, in my meditation;
> Preserve my life from fear of the enemy.
> Hide me from the secret plots of the wicked.
> From the rebellion of the workers of iniquity.
> Who sharpen their tongue like a sword, and bend their
>   bows to shoot their arrows—bitter words.
> That they may shoot in secret at the blameless;
> Suddenly they shoot at him and do not fear.
> They encourage themselves in an evil matter;
> They talk of laying snares secretly;
> "They say, "Who will see them?"
> They devise iniquities;
> "We have perfected a shrewd scheme."
> Both the inward thought and the heart of man are deep.
> But God shall shoot at them with an arrow; suddenly
>   they shall be wounded.
> So he will make them stumble over their own tongue;
> All who see them shall flee away.
> All men shall fear,
> And shall declare the work of God;
> For they shall wisely consider his doing.
> The righteous shall be glad in The Lord, and trust in Him.
> And all the upright in heart shall glory.

Oh, praise the Lord and all those who have put the Bible into written words so we may learn and study in the Word of Our Lord.

The second and last vision I've had to date deals with the second coming. I know and believe the Bible when it says no man will ever know this day in advance. But as Dr. David Jerimiah says, each event casts a foreshadow of things to come. I was suddenly aware again during sleep and watching a woman newscaster on TV. She said, "This bill had absolutely no chance of passing. It was dead on arrival."

I remember thinking at this point, *Why am I thinking of politics? I can't stand to see or hear about these things.* Then I heard outside voices, many of them from all around saying, almost singing over and over, "He is coming. He is coming." Then I had this incredible feeling of overwhelming joy and happiness. This scene ended with a cloudy light coming at me and consuming all of my vision. Is this that shadow that will be cast minutes before our Lord comes to get His church? I'll leave that for you to decide, but for me, I watch the news with added interest!

One can listen to or watch any of the teachers I have listed in this book and hear them talk about the meaning of the book of Revelation and the second coming of our Lord to collect the church. I want to be ready, and joyfully I look forward to the day He comes to get us. Because I have asked for and look forward to His coming, I believe that I was shown this precursor and that I will see and recognize this shadow of things to come. And I believe this will happen in my lifetime. I'm close to being considered old. To my grandchildren I'm ancient, so there's not a lot of time till this happens. Many teachers say that there's nothing left to happen biblically before the Lord comes back. I agree with that statement. How about you? Are you ready today?

Summation

B y grace and through the blood of our Lord Jesus Christ, my entire immediate family is saved. I did not want to give conclusions in this section because I hope this is not the end of our story but merely a summation of all that has transpired so far.

In our troubling world and indeed our own nation of the United States, I believe the Lord is looking for us to be *bold* for Christ. These are the last days before the return of our Lord. Now is the time when all must take action to save our loved ones from the fires of hell. Though our story I viewed myself as standing on a small white cloud close to the ground with Jesus standing behind me with His hand on my shoulder, smiling. Sharmalie, Danielle, and Aaron kept reaching and trying to come up with me, but just as with a real cloud, each time they tried to grab a hold and pull themselves up, their hands just passed through the cloud and could not grab it. It was not until someone reached them with the truth of the Word of the Bible that they confessed with their mouths and believed in their hearts and were saved by the grace of God. Only then could I pull them up. I reached down to pull my family out of the fire one by one, and when they joined me on the cloud, they still smelled of smoke.

If we all just took the position to save our families, think of how full the churches would be, how the population of hell would diminish. That would really tick off the Devil, wouldn't it? It seems as though the hardest thing to do is to challenge the unsaved in conversation, especially when you know them. You may feel like your own knowledge of the Bible is not strong enough or you won't have the right words to convince nonbelievers or skeptics. Let me ask you this: "Do you think they are any more prepared to defend or understand their own thoughts or positions? How do you know that they are not looking for the answers that you already know?" Your own walk to Christ may be what inspires others to come. I pray ours does. To those who are not saved by the blood of Christ and have read this far into our story, you may be looking for the reason to come to Him, and I pray that our story moves many to begin to pursue that walk or gives some the courage to encourage and bring their own families to Christ as well. The Bible states, "Therefore whoever confesses me before men, Him I will also confess before my Father who is in heaven. But whoever denies me before men, Him I will also deny before my Father who is in heaven" (Matthew 10:32–33).

I heard Jack Graham quote another pastor, and this is what he said about talking to unbelievers and being worried about upsetting them: "Where are you going to send them? To a second hell?" Now is the time to talk to unbelievers or believers who have strayed away from the church. Be bold and share the gift that has been freely given to you. Freely give to others your testimony. I love Ephesians, which says, "And for me, that utterance may be given to me, that I may open my mouth boldly to make known the mystery of the gospel. For which I am ambassador in chains; that in it I may speak boldly, as I ought to speak" (Ephesians 6:19–20).

That last phrase is a golden nugget. Take some time to put your own testimonials down in writing by pen or computer, whatever is most comfortable, and tell others how God has been working in your life or has directly affected the outcome of some situations. It may be difficult at first; however, once you begin to write, the Holy Spirit will make things known that were hidden before.

It's now early in the year 2014. Our family story was written not by me but by all of the events that you have just read about. Writing of the book did two things. It clarified how Jesus was really quite active in our lives, and it helped my family become even closer. The kids say they had to learn who I was as a believer in Jesus over time. Well, yes, that's true. I certainly failed at bringing them to Jesus early in life and did not make the kids aware that daddy was being challenged by ghosts and demons and the like. I had to be the shield between them and _it_. I had no problem with my desire to protect them. I was willing to throw myself in front of an oncoming demon train because I knew it could destroy our home, family, support structure, and I knew that it would rob them of a normal childhood in a loving atmosphere.

No matter what was happening between Sharmalie and me or how _it_ was involved, the kids were always shielded. Even though I was fighting the one within my wife at the time, we were never really horrible to each other. The kids thought we never fought, which for the most part is true. When there were the difficult times, which I noted in our story, I knew who the enemy was, and it was not my wife. I took that attitude all along, and that's a big reason we are so in love today and were able to make it beyond the issues of the past. I asked before that you look beyond the normal, words spoken in the heat of the moment, emotions that surface and that you see beyond to what is truly causing the fighting in your family. Can it be spiritual in nature? Not always, but when you become aware by faith through the Word of the Bible, you become a threat. And when attacks on you begin, go to your knees and put it in Jesus' hands first. That guarantees the outcome. These episodes in life may be designed to achieve the goal of getting a person on his or her knees because the individual wasn't there in the first place.

This is when you need to make your own plan. How will you and your family get right with God? When I did this, I prayed that the Lord would show me what needed to be done. For me, those three action points became strongly ingrained in my heart. These were the items that needed to be addressed. No matter what distraction evil put into the mix, we were going to stay the course. Then we just followed the plan to get right with God. You can't travel down an unlit road without the light of the world as your guide. Pray, write a family plan that is Bible-based, communicate it to your family, and then execute that plan. When you are writing your plan, be sure to stay in prayer so that Jesus is involved. Listen for the Holy Spirit in your thoughts. Listen carefully and tell the Lord you're ready to listen.

When you are praying for the development of your plan, keep this thought in mind: When the apostles said to Jesus, "Lord, teach us to pray," Jesus gave them the Lord's Prayer, which in most cases is known by every Christian, but Jesus not only taught them the words of the prayer but also the format for prayer in general. The first lines of the Lord's Prayer give glory to God, "Our Father in heaven, hallowed be your name." And then it gets into asking for "our daily bread" or what we want. *So many of us dive right into the asking part when we pray and never give glory to God first.* We have to remember who we are really talking to here, the Creator of everything, our God.

I like to think that we as Christians have a special function in the world today. For me I want to be the thorn in the skull cap of Satan. I want to be the arrow that pierces him, to be a pain in his existence by proclaiming Jesus as Lord and Savior. If he is so worried about me telling my testimony and he is paying attention to me, maybe that takes his attention off someone else who is close to declaring Jesus as Lord and Savior. I think of myself in this instance as the warrior standing at the front line of the developing charge that's about to take place. We are all lined up and ready to go. The word is given, and we start running toward the Enemy to do battle. We are all wearing our armor of God, and there's me running along with the front wave of believers into battle with Satan and his demons. As I charge, I'm waving my sword and giving a rally cry for the Lord. Only my sword is the Bible, and the battle cry is verses of the Bible, which truly scare the Enemy. *Join our ranks in this war, proclaim Jesus boldly, and set your family on the path to find Him.*

From our family to yours, with love for our brothers and sisters in Christ, we pray for blessings to be placed on your path. We will meet in the clouds during the rapture when our Lord comes to take us home, or we will have an eternity to find each other in heaven. For me it will be right after I'm allowed to go find that wall I was shown!

For your easy reference when the time is right and needed, the sinner's prayer or prayer of salvation, speak this out loud, and believe in your heart the truth of these words, and you will inherit eternal salvation through our Lord Jesus Christ, say *"Lord Jesus, I believe You came into this world and died for my sins. I ask You to come into my heart and soul. I receive You as my Lord and Savior."*

Appendix

The First Gift of Christmas 2012

How strong is your faith? Is it intellectual? What you think you know and believe or is it saving faith, what the Holy Spirit gives through true belief and a strong need to learn. Use the Bible as your main resource. Your trials will come. Here's how to be ready.

True examples of faith include the following:

- Luke 7:2–10
- Matthew 6:30–34
- *Faith is the evidence of things not seen.* Men were on the main floor of the temple, and women were packed in on the upper level. (Women were not allowed on the main floor of the temple.) One little old woman bent over and made it in to the temple upstairs so that she could hear Jesus speak. She was somewhere in the back of the line, and she was not able to see

over the others or be seen by Jesus on the floor below. Jesus suddenly stopped preaching and called for her by name and asked the men to bring her down to the main floor. He chased the demon out by "loosing" the demon from her body and commanded her to be upright, and she was healed. He saw this women not by sight but because her faith was above all those in the temple. Jesus doesn't respond to *need* but to *faith*.

- Are you a doubting Thomas? After Jesus died, Thomas did not believe that He had come back and shown Himself to others and said, "I will believe when I put my hands in His wounds." Jesus let him do this. What will it take to move you to true belief?

- Mummy and Daddy's walk with Christ in belief, our experiences retold and explained.

In times of doubt, consider the following:

- Even John the Baptist had times of doubt, but he went to the source to ask for the answer.

- Remember that Jesus said, "I am the way, the truth and the life, no man comes to the Father but by me."

- The disciples doubted when crossing the sea with Jesus in the boat, he falls asleep and a great storm comes. They woke Jesus, crying out, "Lord, do you not care that we die?" Jesus stood up and said to the sea, "Be calm," and immediately all waves stopped. The winds went away, and the sun came back out. Then they said, "You truly are the Son of God." Your doubts will come be ready to rely on Him.

- Another storm came upon the boat when Jesus remained on land. The apostles fought to exhaustion. Just when all seemed lost, Jesus appeared walking on water. Peter began to walk on water to Jesus. The moment he took his eyes off of Jesus, he began to sink and cried out for Jesus to save him. The lesson is that when you doubt, faith begins to wane. Keep your eyes and heart on Him. He alone can and will change your path if you have faith!

How can you keep your faith strong and growing? Face your doubts with Christ in prayer. Hang around with other believers at church! Spend time in the Bible, reading the Word or hearing it on DavidJerimah.org. Jesus said, "Blessed are those who see and believe, but truly, truly I tell you, truly blessed are those who have not seen and believe." You are saved by grace through faith. Your faith and understanding grows by speaking the Word. The men in your family must be the pastors to your family. It is your commandment and responsibility.

CPSIA information can be obtained at www.ICGtesting.com
Printed in the USA
BVOW03s0926100714

358687BV00001B/2/P